MAKING MISCHIEF

MAKING MISCHIEF

FALL OF THE KINGDOM, RISE OF THE FOOT SOLDIER
by Somalia Seaton

ALWAYS ORANGE
by Fraser Grace

OBERON BOOKS
LONDON

WWW.OBERONBOOKS.COM

First published in 2016 by Oberon Books Ltd
521 Caledonian Road, London N7 9RH
Tel: +44 (0) 20 7607 3637 / Fax: +44 (0) 20 7607 3629
e-mail: info@oberonbooks.com
www.oberonbooks.com

Visit www.oberonbooks.com to read more about all our books and to buy them. You will also find features, author interviews and news of any author events, and you can sign up for e-newsletters so that you're always first to hear about our new releases.

Contents

ABOUT THE ROYAL SHAKESPEARE COMPANY

The Shakespeare Memorial Theatre opened in Stratford-upon-Avon in 1879. Since then the plays of Shakespeare have been performed here, alongside the work of his contemporaries and of modern playwrights. In 1960 the Royal Shakespeare Company was formed, gaining its Royal Charter in 1961.

The founding Artistic Director, Peter Hall, created an ensemble theatre company of young actors and writers. The Company was led by Hall, Peter Brook and Michel Saint-Denis. The founding principles were threefold: the Company would embrace the freedom and power of Shakespeare's work, train and develop young actors and directors and, crucially, experiment in new ways of making theatre. There was a new spirit amongst this post-war generation and they intended to open up Shakespeare's plays as never before.

The impact of Peter Hall's vision cannot be overplayed. In 1955 he premiered Samuel Beckett's *Waiting for Godot* in London, and the result was like opening a window during a storm. The tumult of new ideas emerging across Europe in art, theatre and literature came flooding into British theatre. Hall channelled this new excitement into the setting up of the Company in Stratford. Exciting breakthroughs took place in the rehearsal room and the studio day after day. The RSC became known for exhilarating performances of Shakespeare alongside new masterpieces such as *The Homecoming* and *Old Times* by Harold Pinter. It was a combination that thrilled audiences.

Peter Hall's rigour on classical text became legendary, but what is little known is that he applied everything he learned working on Beckett, and later on Harold Pinter, to his work on Shakespeare, and likewise he applied everything he learned from Shakespeare onto modern texts. This close and exacting relationship between writers from different eras became the fuel which powered the creativity of the RSC.

The search for new forms of writing and directing was led by Peter Brook. He pushed writers to experiment. "Just as Picasso set out to capture a larger slice of the truth by painting a face with several eyes and noses, Shakespeare, knowing that man is living his everyday life and at the same time is living intensely in the invisible world of his thoughts and feelings, developed a method through which we can see at one and the same time the look on a man's face and the vibrations of his brain."

In our 50 years of producing new plays, we have sought out some of the most exciting writers of their generation. These have included: Edward Albee, Howard Barker, Alice Birch, Edward Bond, Howard Brenton, Marina Carr, Caryl Churchill, Martin Crimp, David Edgar, Helen Edmundson, James Fenton, Georgia Fitch, David Greig, Tanika Gupta, Ella Hickson, Dennis Kelly, Tarell Alvin McCraney, Martin McDonagh, Tom Morton-Smith, Rona Munro, Anthony Neilson, Harold Pinter, Phil Porter, Mike Poulton, Mark Ravenhill, Adriano Shaplin, Tom Stoppard, debbie tucker green, Timberlake Wertenbaker, Peter Whelan and Roy Williams.

The Company today is led by Gregory Doran, whose appointment represents a long-term commitment to the disciplines and craftsmanship required to put on the plays of Shakespeare. He, along with Executive Director, Catherine Mallyon, and his Deputy Artistic Director, Erica Whyman, will take forward a belief in celebrating both Shakespeare's work and the work of his contemporaries, as well as inviting some of the most exciting theatre-makers of today to work with the Company on new plays.

The RSC Acting Companies are generously supported by THE GATSBY CHARITABLE FOUNDATION and THE KOVNER FOUNDATION.

The work of the RSC Literary Department is generously supported by THE DRUE HEINZ TRUST.

The RSC is grateful for the significant support of its principal funder, Arts Council England, without which our work would not be possible. Around 75 per cent of the RSC's income is self-generated from Box Office sales, sponsorship, donations, enterprise and partnerships with other organisations.

Supported using public funding by
ARTS COUNCIL ENGLAND

NEW WORK AT THE RSC

We are a contemporary theatre company built on classical rigour. Through an extensive programme of research and development, we resource writers, directors and actors to explore and develop new ideas for our stages, and as part of this we commission playwrights to engage with the muscularity and ambition of the classics and to set Shakespeare's world in the context of our own. This year we have re-opened The Other Place, our studio theatre in Stratford-upon-Avon, which will be a creative home for new work and experimentation.

We invite writers to spend time with us in our rehearsal rooms, with our actors and practitioners. Alongside developing their own plays for our stages, we invite them to contribute dramaturgically to both our main-stage Shakespeare productions and our work for young people. We believe that engaging with living writers and other contemporary theatre makers helps to establish a creative culture within the Company which both inspires new work and creates an ever more urgent sense of enquiry into the classics. Shakespeare was a great innovator and breaker of rules, as well as a bold commentator on the times in which he lived. It is his spirit of 'Radical Mischief' which informs new work at the RSC.

Erica Whyman, Deputy Artistic Director, heads up this strand of the Company's work alongside Pippa Hill as Literary Manager.

MAKING MISCHIEF
'What is unsayable in the 21st century?'

Our writers respond to this challenge with daring explorations of language, race, gender and life in Britain today. Join us in our intimate new theatre space at The Other Place and confront your own assumption about what is taboo in the times we live in.

The *Making Mischief* Festival was first presented by the Royal Shakespeare Company in The Other Place, Stratford-upon-Avon, on 27 July 2016. The cast was as follows:

Fall of the Kingdom, Rise of the Foot Soldier by Somalia Seaton

AISHA	**DONNA BANYA**
CHORUS	**BALLY GILL**
HAWKINS	**LAURA HOWARD**
CHORUS	**TYRONE HUGGINS**
SHABZ	**SYREETA KUMAR**
ARCHIE/CHORUS	**IFAN MEREDITH**

Always Orange by Fraser Grace

AMNA/SHERMEERA	**DONNA BANYA**
NIALL	**SAM COLE**
NO NAME I/PARVENDRA	**BALLY GILL**
DOLORES/JACKIE	**LAURA HOWARD**
FAROUK/MR IBRAHIM	**TYRONE HUGGINS**
RUSHA	**SYREETA KUMAR**
JOE	**IFAN MEREDITH**
HOUIDA/LORNA/NO NAME II	**BIANCA STEPHENS**

Fall of the Kingdom, Rise of the Foot Soldier

Director	**Nadia Latif**
Designer	**Madeleine Girling**
Lighting Designer	**Claire Gerrens**
Sound Designer	**Steven Atkinson**
Voice and Text Work	**Anna McSweeney**
Assistant Director	**Paris Erotokritou**
Casting Director	**Matthew Dewsbury**
Dramaturg	**Pippa Hill**
Production Manager	**Julian Cree**
Costume Supervisor	**Zarah Meherali**
Company Stage Manager	**Julia Wade**
Assistant Stage Managers	**Kezia Beament, Jessica Hardcastle**
Producer	**Claire Birch**

Always Orange

Director	**Donnacadh O'Briain**
Designer	**Madeleine Girling**
Lighting Designer	**Matt Peel**
Sound Designer	**Steven Atkinson**
Movement Director	**Jüri Nael**
Voice and Text Work	**Anna McSweeney**
Assistant Director	**Guy Jones**
Casting Director	**Matthew Dewsbury**
Dramaturg	**Pippa Hill**
Production Manager	**Julian Cree**
Costume Supervisor	**Zarah Meherali**
Company Stage Manager	**Julia Wade**
Assistant Stage Managers	**Kezia Beament, Jessica Hardcastle**
Producer	**Claire Birch**

This text may differ slightly from the play as performed.

THEATRE AT ITS BEST

Support us and make a difference

The RSC is a registered charity. Our aim is to stage theatre at its best, made in Stratford-upon-Avon and shared around the world with the widest possible audience.

We need your support and ask you to become a Member or join our Shakespeare Circle or Patrons Circle to enjoy a closer relationship with the Company. For just £18 per year you will receive advance information and enjoy Priority Booking for all seasons, giving you the chance to be among the first to see our new productions. For further insight into the Company and invites to exclusive events whilst directly funding the work on our stage join our Shakespeare Circle or Patrons Circle from £100 per year.

For more information visit **www.rsc.org.uk/supportus** or call the RSC Membership Office on 01789 403440.

CAST

DONNA BANYA
AISHA/AMNA/SHERMEERA
RSC: *Fall of the Kingdom, Rise of the Foot Soldier*; *Always Orange*.
TRAINED: National Youth Theatre.
THEATRE INCLUDES: *Homegrown* (Site-Specific Theatre); *Good to be Bad* (Artemis Productions); *Pronoun* (National Theatre Connections).

BALLY GILL
CHORUS/NO NAME I/PARVENDRA
RSC: *Fall of the Kingdom, Rise of the Foot Soldier*; *Always Orange*.
TRAINED: Rose Bruford.
THEATRE INCLUDES: *Dinner with Saddam* (Menier Chocolate Factory); *A Local Boy* (Invertigo Theatre).
THEATRE WHILST TRAINING: *The Bureau of Lost Things* (Theatre503); *Table* (Stratford Circus Arts Centre).

SAM COLE
NIALL
RSC: *Always Orange*.
TRAINED: Theatre Workshop.
THEATRE INCLUDES: *Back Down* (Birmingham Rep); *Bashment Housewives* (The Drum).
FILM: *Jawbone*.
RADIO: *Sunny and Shay Show* (Radio WM).

LAURA HOWARD
HAWKINS/DOLORES/JACKIE
RSC: *Fall of the Kingdom, Rise of the Foot Soldier*; *Always Orange*.
THEATRE INCLUDES: *Crushed Shells and Mud* (Southwark Playhouse); *Invincible* (Orange Tree/St James Theatre); *Lost in Yonkers* (Watford Palace); *The Norman Conquests* (Liverpool Playhouse); *Life of Riley*, *Communicating Doors* (Stephen Joseph Theatre); *Two Women* (Theatre Royal Stratford East); *Look Back in Anger* (Northern Stage); *The Blue Room* (Anvil Arts); *Switzerland* (HighTide); *Dracula* (Centerline/English Touring Theatre); *The Hotel in Amsterdam*

(Donmar Warehouse); *Emma* (Good Company Players); *Arcadia* (Chichester Festival Theatre); *The Master Builder*, *The Taming of the Shrew* (English Touring Theatre).
TELEVISION INCLUDES: *Casualty*, *Cuffs*, *The Delivery Man*, *Doctors*, *Young Dracula*, *EastEnders*, Cully Barnaby in *Midsomer Murders*, *Cold Enough for Snow*, *Soldier Soldier*, *Eskimo Day*, *The Bill*, *Covington Cross*, *Queen's Park Story*, *So Haunt Me*.

(Contact Theatre); *Sounds... In Session* (Theatre of Darkness); *The Honey Man* (New Perspectives).
TELEVISION INCLUDES: *Rome*, *The Amazing Mrs Pritchard*, *Holby City*, *Dangerfield*, *Backup*.
FILM INCLUDES: *Run Fat Boy Run*, *Giving Tongue*, *The Absence of War*, *The Last Client*.
RADIO INCLUDES: *The Diary of Adam and Eve*, *Raising the Sage*, *Amsterdam*.

TYRONE HUGGINS
CHORUS/FAROUK/MR IBRAHIM
RSC: *Fall of the Kingdom, Rise of the Foot Soldier*; *Always Orange*; *King Lear*; *Noughts & Crosses*.
THEATRE INCLUDES: *Opening Skinner's Box* (Northern Stage/West Yorkshire Playhouse/Improbable Theatre); Prospero in *The Tempest* (Northern Stage/Oxford Playhouse/Improbable Theatre); *The Honey Man* (Birmingham Rep/Judy Owen Ltd); *Electra* (Old Vic/Sonia Friedman Productions); *I Was a Rat!* (Birmingham Rep/Nottingham Playhouse/New Wolsey/Teatro Kismet); *25/7* (Talking Birds Theatre Company); *Natural Breaks and Rhythms* (TWP/Northampton Theatre); *Of Mice and Men* (Birmingham Rep/Savoy Theatre); *Time and the Room* (Nottingham Playhouse); Sanda in *The Beatification of Area Boy* (West Yorkshire Playhouse); *The Hare Trilogy* (National Theatre); *Woza Albert*, *A Raisin in the Sun*, *Blood Wedding* (Contact Theatre). Devised productions include: *#117 The Birthday Show* (People Show); *Spring's Sprung* (Women & Theatre). As writer: *Choo Choo Ch' Boogie* (Bolton Octagon); *The Carver Chair*

SYREETA KUMAR
SHABZ/RUSHA
RSC: *Fall of the Kingdom, Rise of the Foot Soldier*; *Always Orange*; *Much Ado About Nothing*; *Hamlet*; *Camino Real*; *Midnight's Children*; *Twelfth Night*.
THEATRE INCLUDES: *Dr Blighty* (Nutkhut); *The Husbands* (Kali Theatre); *Red Ladies* (Clod Ensemble); *Haroun and the Sea of Stories* (National Theatre). Syreeta has also worked with London Bubble Theatre Company, Theatre Royal Stratford East, Talawa, Black Mime, Wildcat, Tara Arts and Filter.
TELEVISION INCLUDES: *Apple Tree Yard*, *Lewis*, *Stella*, *Doctors*, *Coronation Street*, *Torchwood*, *Silk*.

IFAN MEREDITH
ARCHIE/CHORUS/JOE
RSC: *Fall of the Kingdom, Rise of the Foot Soldier*; *Always Orange*.
TRAINED: Central School of Speech and Drama.
THEATRE INCLUDES: *Time and the Conways* (Nottingham Playhouse); *Union*, *A Midsummer Night's Dream*, *Living Quarters* (Royal Lyceum, Edinburgh); *Love and Money* (Fresh Target); *PEEP* (Natural Shocks/Edinburgh Festival); *Sexlife/69* (Natural Shocks/Edinburgh Festival); *The Roman Bath* (Arcola/National Theatre of Bulgaria); *Measure for Measure*, *Small Change* (Sherman Cymru); *Mincemeat* (Cardboard Citizens); *Romeo and Juliet* (Middle Temple Hall); *The English Game* (Headlong); *Frankenstein* (Frantic Assembly); *Hamlet* (The Factory); *Romeo and Juliet* (Queen's, Hornchurch); *Mrs Pat* (Theatre Royal, York); *Much Ado About Nothing* (Peter Hall Company); *Then They Came For Me* (Walk Our Talk Productions); *Journey's End* (West End); *The Tempest* (Almeida); *Mrs Warren's Profession* (Manchester Royal Exchange); *A View from the Bridge* (Sheffield Crucible); *Candida* (Bolton Octagon); *Loot* (West Yorkshire Playhouse); *The Accrington Pals* (Embassy Theatre).
TELEVISION INCLUDES: *Titanic*, *Warriors*, *Great Expectations*, *Dr Jekyll & Mr Hyde*, *Sirens*, *The Grand*, *Band of Gold*, *The Mill on the Floss*, *Holby City*, *Murder City*, *The Royal*, *Where the Heart Is*, *Peak Practice*, *A Mind to Kill*, *A Light in the Valley*, *Midsomer Murders*, *Victoria Cross*, *Doctors*, *Dark Matters*, *True Stories: Alexander Graham Bell*.
FILM INCLUDES: *Ripley Under Ground*, *Metroland*.

BIANCA STEPHENS
HOUIDA/LORNA/NO NAME II
RSC: *Always Orange*.
TRAINED: Royal Welsh College of Music and Drama, Identity Drama School, National Youth Theatre.
THEATRE INCLUDES: Lucy in *Blue*, Hellena in *The Rover*, Chris/Bianca in *Narrative*, First Witch in *Macbeth*, Daisy in *In Arabia We'd All Be Kings*, Gloria in *Dogville* (Richard Burton Company); Sopriyia in *E15* (FYSA Theatre).
RADIO: Newsreader in *Dorian Gray* (Big Finish).

CREATIVE TEAM

STEVEN ATKINSON
SOUND DESIGNER
RSC: *Fall of the Kingdom, Rise of the Foot Soldier*; *Always Orange*. Steve is currently a member of the RSC Sound Department.
TRAINED: University of Huddersfield, BA (Hons) Music Production.
WORK INCLUDES: Following training, Steve worked for several years in his native St. Albans as both a theatre technician and later as venue manager. In 2011 he joined the RSC Sound Department for the inaugural season in the redeveloped theatres. Since then he has toured for the RSC several times as Senior Sound Technician, and has taken shows across the UK and installed residencies for RSC productions in Newcastle, the Roundhouse and the Barbican. Most recently, Steve took the *King & Country* season of shows to mainland China, the Hong Kong Arts Festival and the Brooklyn Academy of Music.

PARIS EROTOKRITOU
ASSISTANT DIRECTOR
RSC: *Fall of the Kingdom, Rise of the Foot Soldier*.
TRAINED: RADA (MA Theatre Directing), Athens Drama School (BA Acting), King's College London.
THEATRE INCLUDES: Paris is the Artistic Director of Fresh Target Theatre Ensemble. As Assistant/Associate/Touring Director: *'Tis Pity She's a Whore* (Cheek by Jowl); *Homegrown* (National Youth Theatre); *Yerma* (RADA). As Director: *Wolfgang* (GFCA); *Home Project UK* (Theatre Royal, Stratford East); *Love and Money*, *The Kitchen* (RADA); *Heart of a Dog* (Paravan Proactions); *Nitsa*, *A Respectable Wedding*, *A Slight Risk*, *Contractions*, *New World Order*, *One for the Road*, *Press Conference*, *Precisely*, *The Lover*, *Jack's Master* (Fresh Target Theatre Ensemble). He has worked as an Associate Radar Director at the Bush Theatre in 2013 and has led numerous theatre workshops in Athens, Nicosia and London. In January 2017 he will direct *Scorched* by Wajdi Mouawad at the Cyprus National Theatre.

CLAIRE GERRENS
LIGHTING DESIGNER
RSC: *Fall of the Kingdom, Rise of the Foot Soldier*; *The Ant and the Cicada*; *Revolt. She said. Revolt again*. Claire joined the RSC Lighting Department in 2010.
TRAINED: Technical Theatre Arts, RADA.
THEATRE INCLUDES: In Claire's six years at Stratford she has worked on a number of productions across the Courtyard, RST, Swan and Roundhouse but her highlights so far include: Lighting Programmer and re-lighting on *A Midsummer Night's Dream: A Play for the Nation*, Lighting Programmer on *The Tempest* with Little Angel Theatre Company (Stratford); Lighting Programmer on *Julius Caesar* (Stratford/UK and international tour); Lighting Programmer and re-lighting on *The Rape of Lucrece* (Stratford/UK, Ireland and international tour); Lighting Programmer on *Cardenio* (Stratford); Lighting Programmer on *Wendy & Peter Pan* (Stratford, 2013 and 2015).

MADELEINE GIRLING
DESIGNER
RSC: *Fall of the Kingdom, Rise of the Foot Soldier*; *Always Orange*; *The Ant and the Cicada*; *Revolt. She said. Revolt again*. Between 2013 and 2014 Madeleine worked in a one-year Design Assistant position.
TRAINED: Madeleine trained in Theatre Design at the Royal Welsh College of Music and Drama, graduating with a First Class Honours, and receiving the Lord Williams Memorial Prize for Design in 2012. In 2013 she was a winner in the Linbury Prize for Stage Design for her collaboration with Nottingham Playhouse.
THEATRE INCLUDES: *Julie* (Northern Stage); *Right Now* (Ustinov Studio/Bush/Traverse); *A Skull in Connemara* (Nottingham Playhouse); *The Harvest* (Ustinov Studio/Soho Theatre); *Little Light* (Orange Tree); *The Chronicles of Kalki* (Gate); *Time and the Conways*, *Arcadia* (Nottingham Playhouse); *Gardening for the Unfulfilled and Alienated* (Undeb Theatre); *Tender Napalm*, *How to Curse* (BOVTS

Director's Showcase); *A Welshman's Guide to Breaking Up* (Boyo Productions); *Hey Diddle Diddle* (Bristol Old Vic); *The Cagebirds* (LAMDA Director's Showcase); *The Life After* (BOV Young Company); *Blood Wedding* (RWCMD Burton Company).

FRASER GRACE
PLAYWRIGHT
RSC: *Always Orange*, *Breakfast with Mugabe*.
Fraser's first play for the RSC was *Breakfast with Mugabe*, which won the John Whiting Best Play Award in 2006, directed by Antony Sher. The production transferred to the Soho Theatre and then to the West End. The play has subsequently been produced at the Ustinov Studio, Bath, and in the USA, where it was nominated for Best Play in the Off-Broadway Stage Awards 2014.
Other plays include *Perpetua* (Verity Bargate Award), *Gifts of War*, *Who Killed Mr Drum?* (with Sylvester Stein), *Frobisher's Gold*, *The Lifesavers* (nominated for TMA Award, Best New Play), *King David*, *Man of Blood*, and *Kalashnikov: In the Woods by the Lake*. Fraser has directed the University of Birmingham's Masters course in playwriting since 2011, and is co-author (with Clare Bayley) of *Playwriting: A Writers' & Artists' Companion*, published by Bloomsbury in 2016. All of Fraser's plays, including *Always Orange*, are published by Oberon Books.

PIPPA HILL
DRAMATURG
RSC: *Fall of the Kingdom, Rise of the Foot Soldier*; *Always Orange*; *Don Quixote*; *Hecuba*; *Oppenheimer*; *The Christmas Truce*; *The Roaring Girl*; *The Ant and the Cicada*; *I Can Hear You*; *Wendy & Peter Pan*; *The Empress*; *The Thirteen Midnight Challenges of Angelus Diablo*; *Here Lies Mary Spindler*.
Pippa Hill is the Literary Manager at the RSC and oversees the commissioning and development of all of the company's new plays, adaptations and translations. She also works closely with the creative teams preparing the texts for the classical repertoire. She was previously the Literary Manager at Paines Plough running three nationwide writing initiatives designed to identify and develop new playwrights.

GUY JONES
ASSISTANT DIRECTOR
RSC: *Always Orange*; *Cymbeline*.
TRAINED: University of Manchester, National Theatre Director's Course.
THEATRE INCLUDES: *The Winter's Tale*, *Twelfth Night* (Orange Tree); *Disnatured* (Shakespeare in Shoreditch Festival); *Spokesong* (Finborough Theatre); *On Reflection* (Southbank Centre); *Caterpillar* (Bush); *What Will Survive of Us* (Islington Community Theatre/National Theatre); *No Wonder* (Manchester Library Theatre/National Student Drama Festival). As Assistant Director: Resident Assistant Director at Finborough Theatre; *Touched* (North Wall/Latitude); *Madam Cassie's Cabaret* (HMP Styal). Guy was a finalist for the JMK Award 2016. As a dramaturg Guy is Literary Associate at Orange Tree and has been an Associate Artist at Islington Community Theatre. Dramaturgy credits elsewhere include: *There There, Stranger* (Sadler's Wells); *The Armour* (Langham Hotel).

NADIA LATIF
DIRECTOR
RSC: *Fall of the Kingdom, Rise of the Foot Soldier*.
THEATRE INCLUDES: As Director: *Octagon* (Arcola); *Homegrown* (NYT, site specific); *Even Stillness Breathes Softly Against a Brick Wall* (Soho); *Saved* (Drama Centre); *but i cd only whisper* (Arcola/Lincoln Centre, NYC); *Carrot* (Latitude/Theatre503); *Coalition*, *Wild Horses*, *Slaves* (Theatre503); *Hand Me Down* (Almeida Theatre Projects, devised piece); *The Ballad of Crazy Paola* (Arcola); *In the Heart of America*, *The Daughter in Law* (RADA). As Assistant/

Associate Director: *Decade* (Headlong); *The Great Game* (Tricycle); *Chain Play II*, *The Homecoming* (Almeida); *Wuthering Heights* (RADA. Co-adaptor); *I Like Mine With a Kiss* (Bush). Nadia was an Associate Director at Theatre503 from 2009-2011.

ANNA McSWEENEY
TEXT & VOICE WORK
RSC: *Fall of the Kingdom, Rise of the Foot Soldier*; *Always Orange*. **Anna is a member of the Artist Support Department.**
Anna is a voice practitioner with an MA in Voice Studies from the prestigious Central School of Speech and Drama. She also has a BA in Acting from Guildhall School of Music and Drama and a BA in English Literature from Warwick University. Prior to starting her role at the RSC, Anna has worked as a voice coach at a variety of London drama schools including Drama Centre, Mountview and Italia Conti.

JÜRI NAEL
MOVEMENT DIRECTOR
RSC: *Always Orange*.
WORK INCLUDES: Jüri has created original choreography for over 80 theatre productions in Estonia, Finland, Sweden, Germany and the UK. As Choreographer: *Jesus Christ Superstar*, *Evita*, *Chess* (Theatre Vanemuine); *Les Misérables*, *Miss Saigon* (Tallinn City Hall/tour production in Germany); *West Side Story* (Helsinki City Theatre, Karlstad Opera, Theatre Vanemuine); *Cabaret* (Theatre Vanalinnastuudio); *Grease*, *Fame*, *Cinderella*, *The Phantom of the Opera* (Tallinn City Hall); *Rent* (Malvius Productions); *Hairspray* (Helsinki City Theatre); *Little Shop of Horrors* (Estonian Drama Theatre); *Sugar* (Vaasa Theatre/Luleo Theatre); *Tanz der Vampire*, *La Cage aux Folles* (Smithbridge Productions); *Andrew Lloyd Webber Gala* (Tallinn Song Festival Grounds). As Movement Director: *Rotterdam* (Trafalgar Studios); *The Brothers Karamazov*, *Reigen*, *Masked*, *Penetrator*, *Get to Know the World*, *Nocturnal* (RADA); *The Suicide*, *Pericles*, *Iphigenia in Aulis*, *Filth*, *El Dorado* (Theatre NO99); *Romeo and Juliet*, *The Lieutenant of Inishmore* (Estonian Drama Theatre); *Animal Farm* (Tallinn City Theatre); *The Hour We Knew Nothing of Each Other* (Thalia Theatre Hamburg); *Eugénie Grandet* (Edinburgh Fringe).

DONNACADH O'BRIAIN
DIRECTOR
RSC: *Always Orange*. **Donnacadh was Assistant Director on the multi-award winning Histories Cycle and *The Canterbury Tales*.**
THEATRE INCLUDES: Donnacadh is Artistic Director of Natural Shocks. For Natural Shocks: created the unique cross art form pop-up theatre PEEP (Edinburgh Fringe/Latitude Festival); *Rotterdam*, *Mathematics of the Heart* (Theatre503); *Between Life and Nowhere* (Theatre Delicatessen); *The Early Bird* (Finborough Theatre/Project, Dublin); *A Midsummer Night's Dream*, *The Comical Mysteries* (Civic Theatre Tallaght); *Twelfth Night* (Crypt, Dublin Castle). Other recent projects include: *The Easter Rising* and *Thereafter, Lesere* (Jermyn Street); *The Tempest* (BOVTS/ Redgrave Theatre); *The Poet, the Lover and the Lunatic*, *Anonymity* (National Portrait Gallery); *Blue Stockings* (Tobacco Factory, Bristol); *Eugénie Grandet* (Assembly, Edinburgh Fringe); *From Both Hips*, *Mercury Fur* (RADA); *Betrayal* (Theatro dell'orologio, Rome); *King Lear* (Second Age); *Richard III* (Southwark Playhouse. Better Bankside Shakespeare Award winner); *Hush* (Edinburgh Fringe). The transfer of his production of *Rotterdam* opens at Trafalgar Studios in July, and a transfer of *My World Has Exploded a Little Bit* (Natural Shocks) plays at Underbelly as part of this year's Edinburgh Fringe.
OTHER: Donnacadh directs and teaches acting at major drama schools, including RADA, LAMDA and Bristol Old Vic Theatre School, and was Associate Fellow at Warwick University's CAPITAL Centre while Assistant Director at the RSC.

MATT PEEL
LIGHTING DESIGNER

RSC: *Always Orange*. Matt is a Senior Lighting Technician in the RSC Lighting Department. As Lighting Designer: *Pericles*, *Song of Songs*, *Musicals Celebration*, *Silence* (TOP/Arcola); *Dr Foster* (TOP/Menier Chocolate Factory). Relighting on: *Twelfth Night*, *The Tempest* (Roundhouse); *The Canterbury Tales* (tour); *King Lear* (international tour).

THEATRE INCLUDES: As Lighting Designer: *Eden's Empire* (Finborough). Relighting: *Arthur and George* (Birmingham Rep). As Assistant Lighting Designer: *Disney's The Lion King* (Scheveningen/UK tour); *Mamma Mia!* (Moscow).

SOMALIA SEATON
PLAYWRIGHT

RSC: *Fall of the Kingdom, Rise of the Foot Soldier*.

Somalia is a British writer and actress of Jamaican and Nigerian parentage, born and raised in South-East London. She trained at East 15 Acting School on the BA (Hons) contemporary theatre course. She is also Artistic Director of No Ball Games Allowed, creating work with young people at its core. Her debut play *Crowning Glory* was shortlisted for the 2014 Alfred Fagon Award. Currently she is on the Talawa Writers' Programme under commission to both the Talawa Theatre Company and the Bush Theatre. She is also on attachment and under commission to Clean Break, The Yard and the RSC.

These two courageous plays were commissioned in 2016 in response to the provocation **'What is unsayable in the 21st Century?'**. 400 years since Shakespeare died, and in a year when the RSC also presented ground-breaking productions of *Hamlet*, *King Lear*, *Cymbeline* and *The Tempest*, it seemed imperative to ask our living writers to be as bold, inventive and truthful as these great investigations of power and democracy encourage us to be. Fraser Grace and Somalia Seaton have grasped this challenge with exhilarating honesty, laying bare some of the most uncomfortable aspects of being alive in the United Kingdom now and, in two very different ways, they do this with an elegant and determined theatricality. It is perhaps the artist's most urgent responsibility – to disrupt, to perturb, to disconcert in order to reveal new ways of imagining the world – to make serious mischief. I hope these plays encourage us all to see a little differently.

Erica Whyman, Deputy Artistic Director, July 2016

FALL OF THE KINGDOM, RISE OF THE FOOT SOLDIER

Thank you to Camilla Stanger, Marsha Garrick, Melon, Dad and many others.

Much gratitude to Pippa Hill, Collette McCarthy and the entire Literary team.

The force that is Ms Nadia Latif – nuff love.

Foreword

The journey to write this play has been one of mixed emotions.

I don't have all the answers.

What I do know is this;

We must get angry. We must stay angry. We must get organised.

Anger without strategy is futile.

Above all else we must connect, hear and protect each other.

Silence is not an option. It is in fact complicitness.

We are more powerful than we know.

Collectively.

SS, 2016

Characters

AISHA – Black British – 17, small but mighty. A leader. Comes from an economically middle-class family, with working-class roots.

ARCHIE – White English – 41, middle class, working-class roots. Likes you to know it. Lived in London much of his life. Originally from just outside.

HAWKINS – White English – 39. Middle class from Surrey. Lived in London since graduating from University.

SHABZ – Pakistani British – 40s. Londoner, born and raised.

CHORUS – A chorus of 3. Mixed ages, mixed ethnicities. Should be played be an all-female chorus or an all-male chorus.

NOTES

Where / appears, an overlap is noted.

Where … Appears at the end of the line it is to
note a line interrupted.

Where … Appears in the middle of lines, it is to
note a character finding their thoughts.

THE CHORUS

Choral lines are to be divided to suit the rhythm
developed by the company.

THE WORLD

Set in London. The belly of our beast.
Heightened and dangerous.

A time not too far in the future.

Light rain falls.

CHORUS enter holding a large St. George flag. Plant it in the ground.

CHORUS: *This is our England!*

> Red
>
> white
>
> *and* the blue.
> Rain sleet
>
> and hail but her heart's forever true!
> *This is our England!*
> Steak and kidney pies,
>
> mash with bloody gravy and mint sauce!
> Where we once knew the name of the man at the chippy
> and he knew ya cousin George!
>
> Where Sundays arrive with ya nan stocking you with extra
> Yorkshire puds!
>
> Where she married my grandad and gave him seven
> mucky sorts.
>
> Where *he* taught my dad how to kick a ball,
>
> and he went on to teach me an' all.
>
> *This is our England!*
> With summers spent snogging pretty girls in frilly skirts,
>
> getting slapped for putting our hands down Busty Nancy's
> pinafore!
>
> Where my mates Ollie and Charlie first got knocked off
> their bikes! Where we'd throw conkers at the pikes
>
> and Mum would force us to go back and apologise!
> Where the milk man would leave the milk by your front
> door and you knew ya postman Mike,

with his wife Tash

and their ugly little shites.
This is our England!

Red
white
and the blue.

Men of wisdom men of honour, our hearts are made of it all!

Where our daughters are 'spos'd to run freely, and our sons taught to protect them an' all.

Where our daughters can't run freely and our sons are persecuted for standing up for their rights.

Where we pledge our allegiance to the Queen

and she lets them tear our Great Kingdom apart!

Where I'm told I can fight for Queen and Kingdom

but I can't be proud of my bloodline

Where political correctness is causing our country irreversible scars

and the government is a bloody farce.

But,
This is our England!
This is our England!
This is our England!
And we're gonna fight you for her 'til the day we die!

Thunder.
Rain beats down.
Day turns to night.
Makes way off to battle.
HAWKINS and ARCHIE can be seen running back in the rain.
We are surrounded by news visibly and audibly. The sound of
fear-mongering politicians goes through us.

SCENE 2

Heavy rain.

Evening.

HAWKINS' flat – Modern, plush. In a generic gentrified part of London.

(Sally) HAWKINS – rushes in out of the rain after a date with partner ARCHIE.

ARCHIE – fumbles around, drunk.

HAWKINS enters first throwing her coat down followed by ARCHIE who finds the nearest seat. Pulls unsuccessfully at his boot.

HAWKINS: You should have said thank you

ARCHIE: It was cold and it was spongy / no thank yoous for spongy food…

HAWKINS: Spongy? Well mine wasn't spongy it was delicious

ARCHIE: Oh behave yourself….

HAWKINS: I loved it….

ARCHIE: It was disgusting…

HAWKINS: You're disgusting…

ARCHIE: You love me…

HAWKINS: It wasn't his fault…

ARCHIE: And it's not mine!

HAWKINS: You were obscenely rude

ARCHIE: I was honest

HAWKINS: No…

ARCHIE: Yes…

HAWKINS: Definitely rude….

ARCHIE: He'll remember his place next time….

HAWKINS: Archie!

ARCHIE: I'm joking!

HAWKINS: No you're not

ARCHIE: Who cares…

HAWKINS: I care…

ARCHIE: Too much…

HAWKINS: I do not

ARCHIE: You do

HAWKINS: I just don't want people thinking I'm rude

ARCHIE: I rest my case

HAWKINS: You don't have a case!

ARCHIE: There are worse customers than me

> *He fumbles.*

HAWKINS: You need water

> *She gets some.*

ARCHIE: I do not!
  Maybe

> *Hands it to him.*

HAWKINS: Take it

> *She watches him drink.*

ARCHIE: I'll say thank you next time

HAWKINS: You won't

ARCHIE: Probably not

HAWKINS: You're no good on whisky

ARCHIE: Vicious lies

HAWKINS: Clearly

> *He watches her clear the room.*

ARCHIE: Come here

> *She knows that tone.*

HAWKINS: I'm tired tonight…

ARCHIE: Sally…

HAWKINS: No

   Thank you.

ARCHIE: He's waking up…

HAWKINS: Good for him

ARCHIE: Sally Elizabeth Hawkins….

   She smirks.

HAWKINS: Don't!

 Don't call me that

ARCHIE: Does it make you a little shy?

HAWKINS: Piss off!

ARCHIE: Does it make you want to bounce on my lap

   She doesn't move.

 What if I do a little dance for you?

HAWKINS: Have you peed a bit?

ARCHIE: I'll try anything once

HAWKINS: Fuck off

ARCHIE: Sit on my lap come on!

HAWKINS: You sound like an old pervert

ARCHIE: Sit on my lap Sally Elizabeth Hawkins

   Sings.

 Mustang Sally

HAWKINS: No!

ARCHIE: …Mustang Sally now baybay…

HAWKINS: The song doesn't even bloody go like that you
   buffoon!

He continues.

ARCHIE: …I think you better bring your Mustang…(no) I think you better bring your mustang back arooooooound…

HAWKINS: Are you done?

He hums and gyrates his way over to her.

ARCHIE: Isn't it working?

HAWKINS: No Archie

Beat.

ARCHIE: You are so beautiful when you get all serious

HAWKINS: Doesn't help my dishes I'm afraid

ARCHIE: I like your arse too if it's any consolation?

HAWKINS: It's not!

ARCHIE: Juicy

HAWKINS: Piss off Archie

ARCHIE: Big…juicy…tasty jelly bum bum

HAWKINS: JELLY BUM BUM?!!

ARCHIE: Jelly bum bum!

He stands to chase her, she anticipates.

He heads towards her. She bolts.

HAWKINS: Piss off! You can piss right off!

ARCHIE: Sure?

HAWKINS: Archie!

ARCHIE: I love you

He approaches.

HAWKINS: That's fantastic

ARCHIE: Feeling ticklish?

HAWKINS: If you touch me… so help me God I will scratch your eyes out!

ARCHIE: I love it when you talk like that

HAWKINS: This is not funny!

ARCHIE: Then why are you laughing?

HAWKINS: Because you're a buffoon!

ARCHIE: I'm your buffoon!

He almost catches her.

HAWKINS: Look at your belly!

ARCHIE: Oi!

HAWKINS: Jelly belly!

ARCHIE: It is not!

HAWKINS: Don't like it do you

ARCHIE: You do though!

HAWKINS: Your breath smells like stale whisky

ARCHIE: Liar

HAWKINS: It does!

ARCHIE: I'm going to kiss you!

HAWKINS: You're not!

Almost catches her again.

And I'm not just beautiful

ARCHIE: This is true

HAWKINS: I'm intelligent

ARCHIE: Yes you are

HAWKINS: …and beautiful

ARCHIE: …and it's sexy

He keeps approaching.

HAWKINS: Stay away from me!

ARCHIE: You don't mean that!

HAWKINS: Anyone would think you were sex starved!

ARCHIE: I am sex starved!

HAWKINS: Go home Archie!

He stops.

ARCHIE: Make me

HAWKINS: I mean it

ARCHIE: You're unkind tonight

HAWKINS: I'm not trying to be

ARCHIE: Well you are

HAWKINS: Don't say that

ARCHIE: It's true

HAWKINS: To be honest I can't get what your mother said out
of my mind

ARCHIE: She had too much to drink you know that

HAWKINS: I don't think that's it

ARCHIE: Of course it is

HAWKINS: I just think…

ARCHIE: You do that too much…

HAWKINS: I…I think too much?

ARCHIE: Yeah, you bloody do

HAWKINS: What? Now I'm not allowed to use my brain / Is
that it?

ARCHIE: I never said that

HAWKINS: Well technically / you did….

ARCHIE: My mother made a joke…

HAWKINS: I don't think it was a joke

ARCHIE: Well it was

HAWKINS: Fine…

ARCHIE: And you need to lighten up

HAWKINS: Well I don't feel particularly light at this precise moment

ARCHIE: I could help with that if you would stop bringing my mother up when I'm trying to seduce you

She smirks.

HAWKINS: Archie I'm serious!

ARCHIE: So am I!

HAWKINS: It's on my mind

ARCHIE: She meant nothing by it

HAWKINS: Well I'm not ready…

ARCHIE: Fine…

HAWKINS: We're not ready

ARCHIE: Also fine….

HAWKINS: We don't even live together…

ARCHIE: Well let's / change that?

HAWKINS: And then there's my mother… what? No, why change that?

ARCHIE: So we're more ready

HAWKINS: But you don't want kids

ARCHIE: Could do

HAWKINS: Could do?

ARCHIE: Whatever you want

HAWKINS: Whatever I want?

ARCHIE: Yeah

HAWKINS: It's as simple as that

ARCHIE: Yeah! Why not?

HAWKINS: Like a new handbag / that's ridiculous

ARCHIE: If you want a baby… Let's have a baby

HAWKINS: But…

ARCHIE: I love you

Beat

HAWKINS: Well, I don't know how to take all of this

ARCHIE: Because…you think too much

HAWKINS: Maybe I don't want one

ARCHIE: Then we won't have one

HAWKINS: Again, just like that

ARCHIE: Whatever makes you happy

HAWKINS: Right, okay… well… I mean I haven't achieved nearly a fraction…

ARCHIE: Sally?

HAWKINS: Yes

ARCHIE: Let's fuck!

HAWKINS: Archie!

Seriously! Stop it!

ARCHIE: You need to chill out

HAWKINS: I do not

ARCHIE: You do

HAWKINS: I'm not where I thought I would be at this point in my life and…and when your mother says things like that…

ARCHIE: It was a joke woman

HAWKINS: Well it wasn't funny…

ARCHIE: Sally…

HAWKINS: It just reminds me that I'm only an English
teacher…

ARCHIE: People need to learn English….

HAWKINS: In a school I hate…

ARCHIE: With students you love…

HAWKINS: I should be doing more…

ARCHIE: What do you want?

HAWKINS: I don't know

     Laughs.

I don't know

ARCHIE: You do know

HAWKINS: Really?

ARCHIE: Yes / you always do

HAWKINS: I just don't…

ARCHIE: Aright! Enough now.

HAWKINS: Yes sir!

ARCHIE: You…you listen here
We've had a good night, had a fair bit to drink and I think
it's time you let me take you into that bedroom…

HAWKINS: Oh you do now?

ARCHIE: Hold on!

HAWKINS: Okay…

ARCHIE: I won't even touch you…

HAWKINS: Liar

ARCHIE: I'll just let you nestle in on my chest or something,
make you feel all warm and gooey, deal?

     Beat.

HAWKINS: You make me a bit sick in my mouth

ARCHIE: Made you smile though

HAWKINS: Face spasm actually

ARCHIE: Kiss me

HAWKINS: Come here then

ARCHIE: You come here

HAWKINS: Don't make me change my mind

> *He walks over. Wraps his arms around her. Kisses her hard.
> She gives into it. Then pulls away. He resists. Bites her lip.
> She pushes him with force.*

Fucksake Arch!

> *He lets go and stares into her.*

ARCHIE: Sorry!

HAWKINS: That fuckin' hurt

> *Pushes him again.*

ARCHIE: Alright!

> *He approaches.*
>
> *She pushes him again.*
>
> *He approaches.*
>
> *She pushes him again.*

Kiss me!

> *He kisses her.*

Kiss me!!!

> *He kisses her.*

HAWKINS: No!!!

> *He kisses her.*

ARCHIE: Now!!!!

HAWKINS: No!!!!

She's already in fits of laughter.

ARCHIE: You know what I'm going to do

HAWKINS: Archie

Before she can get her words her he grabs her and tickles her into hysterics.

Arrrgh!!! Okay!!! Okay!!!

Their laughter turns into kissing. He throws her down. They fall to the floor. They kiss and undress frantically.

Three loud knocks can be heard from the outside door. They ignore it at first.

More knocks.

ARCHIE groans.

ARCHIE: Are you kidding me?

HAWKINS: Ignore it

They continue.

Knocks start again frantically.

HAWKINS forces herself up and begins to cover up.

ARCHIE: What are you putting that on for?

HAWKINS: So I can get the door!

ARCHIE: No! Don't do that!

HAWKINS: It's probably him upstairs locked out again

ARCHIE: Let them call a locksmith then…

HAWKINS: It's fine

HAWKINS makes her way over to the door.

ARCHIE: It could be a bloody lost toddler for all I care!

Knocks stop.

HAWKINS looks through the window.

HAWKINS: My God…

ARCHIE: What?

> *She opens the door*
>
> *AISHA,17 walks straight past them and enters the living room. Her hands and clothes covered in blood. Stands. Possessed.*

HAWKINS: Aisha?

> *No reply.*

Aisha?

> *No reply.*

Are you hurt?

> *No reply.*

Does your mother know where you are darling?

ARCHIE: Sally…

HAWKINS: I know

ARCHIE: You do?

HAWKINS: Look at her

> *Beat.*

Aisha darling?

ARCHIE: How on earth does she know where you live?

HAWKINS: Not now…

ARCHIE: You're not thinking straight

HAWKINS: Will you just… will just shut up

> *Beat.*

Aisha I need you to speak to me…okay?

> *No reply.*

Archie get me that chair

ARCHIE: No

HAWKINS: Now

ARCHIE: What are you doing Sally?

HAWKINS: Aisha you have a lot of blood on you

ARCHIE: Aisha are you hurt?

> *She does not respond.*

HAWKINS: We…we should call her parents before anything else, we should…need to call her parents

ARCHIE: No we call the police, now

HAWKINS: If this was my child…

ARCHIE: For Christ' sake think straight!

HAWKINS: I'm trying

ARCHIE: Right Aisha are you hurt?

> *ARCHIE moves suddenly for his phone.*
>
> *AISHA screams and makes for him with the bat.*

Sally call the police

HAWKINS: Aisha look at me!

ARCHIE: Call the police!

HAWKINS: Lower the bat sweetheart

> *She considers.*

AISHA: I don't want him to do that Miss

HAWKINS: Okay

AISHA: I…I don't want him to do that

HAWKINS: Okay darling

> *Beat.*

Go on…lower the bat

> *AISHA slowly turns to face her.*

It's okay…

> *AISHA lowers.*

Are you hurt darling?

> *AISHA nods.*

Can I take a look at you?

> *HAWKINS slowly approaches her, AISHA softens. ARCHIE watches on. As HAWKINS makes contact with AISHA she flinches away.*

ARCHIE: Sally get away from her

HAWKINS: Aisha you're okay here

> *She raises bat again. Backs away from HAWKINS. She's unsettled once more.*

AISHA: I want him…away…I want him gone

HAWKINS: Okay darling

ARCHIE: No one's going to hurt you….

AISHA: Don't talk to me….

HAWKINS: Shut up…

ARCHIE: Put the bat down…

AISHA: Stop talking to me…

HAWKINS: Archie….

AISHA: Make him stop talking to me…

ARCHIE: I'm not going to hurt you…

HAWKINS: Shut up….

AISHA: Get on your knees

> *Beat.*

> *ARCHIE moves once more and AISHA swings the bat in his direction again.*

GET ON YOUR KNEES NOW!

HAWKINS: Do as she says

ARCHIE: Are you insane?

AISHA: Get on your knees

HAWKINS: For Christ' sake do it!

> *Beat*

ARCHIE: I'm not going to hurt you Aisha

> *She begins swinging the bat around in ARCHIE's direction.*

AISHA: Now!

> *He drops to his knees and puts his arms in the air.*

ARCHIE: I'm down! I'm down!

AISHA: Who's here?

HAWKINS: Just us…it's…it's just us

AISHA: I…

HAWKINS: You're safe here

AISHA: My grandad…he will wake up if I don't come home

HAWKINS: He's staying with your parents?

AISHA: He likes to know we are all home

HAWKINS: Okay darling

AISHA: I…I can't go home

HAWKINS: It's okay

AISHA: My battery died
I tried to turn it on it wouldn't go on, my phone wouldn't
go on and I couldn't use it…I couldn't call

HAWKINS: Aisha, will you let me help you?

> *No reply.*

Shall we get you cleaned up?

AISHA: I didn't mean

Beat.

HAWKINS: Didn't mean what darling?

No reply.

Aisha you have a lot of blood on you
Is it yours?

ARCHIE slowly starts to get up.

AISHA: Why is he moving? I don't want him to move, I want
him to stay down there

HAWKINS: Archie stay down...

ARCHIE: We need to get you home....

HAWKINS: Enough...

ARCHIE: We are going to get you / home

AISHA: I don't want him to talk to me...

To ARCHIE.

HAWKINS: Stop

ARCHIE: I will get you home Aisha, no police okay? /
Whatever you have done...

HAWKINS: Shut up, stop talking / you're making...

AISHA: He looked at me like I wasn't human, like I didn't
bleed the same blood like I didn't have blood pumping
through my veins, like my life was worthless, like I was
worthless.... His fist kept... kept pounding and pounding
and pounding and pounding ...the sky was spinning and
the air felt thick and my lungs couldn't feel air, the hairs
on my arms couldn't feel the wind anymore and I couldn't
catch my breath and I wanted him to stop but he wouldn't
stop.... It fell out of his po...po...pocket and I grabbed it
so tight and I cut my hand but I couldn't stop...I...I didn't
want to stop, I didn't want to stop and my hands kept
going and I couldn't feel them anymore they didn't belong
to me they were not mine anymore and then he wasn't
moving and I couldn't breathe... my battery's dead...

She drops the bat, she can't catch her breath.

HAWKINS: Archie call the police

SCENE 3

A rally.

CHORUS: We are a democracy.

A society of tolerance.

A society able to make our own decisions in the world.

A Nation that I am optimistic can one day start re-engaging with the common wealth.

A nation with soul

A nation with pride

A nation with history.

Now, at the core of British values we hold sovereignty and the rule of law at the forefront of our minds.

We are honest

Hard working

Enterprising people.

The history of our Great Nation has long been respected by our allies, in the face of adversity we have shown the world that we unite

That we show our enemies strength

That we will stand firm in the increasing face of terror from those that wish to change the face of all that we have worked for.

But, Britain is changing.
It will continue to change

We are welcoming of this change

but not at the cost of the spirit and the heritage of our
Great Nation.

A nation that has willingly lent its wealth

its culture

and its heart

to less fortunate areas of the world.

Thee honourable member
with his big ideals would have us follow him into his pit of
doom.

Over there youth unemployment is up by 50%

People have been driven to humiliation and desperation

and desperate people do desperate things.

Is that what we want?

For our children?
For their children?
For our legacy?

We don't want that here.

Surely.

That cannot be our story

that cannot be our reality here,

we are a democracy.
We have seen our friend over there, angry, unable to
control his temper, anti-British to his fingertips, exercising
his political fanaticism.

Is that what we want?

A leader the Great British people didn't vote for? Making
decisions for the real people that matter in our country,
without a democratic election? Is that who we have
become?

Surely only a third world country

a banana of a country

could want this type of leader, surely?

A Europe that seeks to be a global super power

We don't want it.

We don't need it.

We reject it.

Right now we are on a lifeboat, at the side of the Titanic, the Titanic that you have boarded and led off towards economic disaster

And we want off.

We want our freedom back

Our independence back.

Freedom for our Great country
Freedom for the labourer working all the hours God gives to ensure some sort of security for his family in a hostile environment over run by immigrants who are allowed to roam in and out of our borders as they please, exhausting our benefits.

Freedom from those that come and disrespect and enforce their beliefs on our land.

I won't allow it.

We can't allow it.

This has to stop.

We need our liberty back

Our democracy back

It is going to happen

It must happen

Perhaps by force.

We will gain our Nation back.

A new democratic revolution that wants a Europe of change.

We are therefore at war.

The barriers have been breached

The guns have been drawn.

Make no mistake Ladies and Gentlemen, we are at war, on home soil.

With enemies who sound

Just like us.

Eat

Just like us.

Frequent the same spaces

Just like us.

What will you do to keep your children safe

To keep their futures safe

To keep their children's children safe?

Will you stand back,

Silent

Complicit

Scared?

Or will you fight. Will you take off the safety catch and fire when the enemy crosses your path.

Will you send them back in their boxes, burnt and shrivelled so their families know who we are?

Will you stand up and be counted?

The time has come for us to pull together

To speak out

To unite.

At the core of British values we hold mutual respect and tolerance of different faiths and beliefs at the forefront of all we stand for as a nation.

But it's not enough.

I call upon you to think wisely

To think carefully

To think of your families

And take your country back.

SCENE 4

The cage.

AISHA a student, sits writing. HAWKINS watches on.

HAWKINS: Time

> *AISHA continues writing.*

Time Aisha

> *She stops, looks up, continues writing and throws her pencil down.*

AISHA: Done

> *HAWKINS collects her paper.*

HAWKINS: How was that?

AISHA: Alright.

HAWKINS: Just alright?

AISHA: Life-changing actually

HAWKINS: Really?

AISHA: No

HAWKINS: You looked like you breezed through

AISHA: Could say that

HAWKINS: Well we've got a little bit of time left so / perhaps…

AISHA: I'm done though

HAWKINS: I don't make the rules I'm afraid

AISHA: Cool

> *HAWKINS looks on from her desk. AISHA taps her foot and keeps her eyes low.*

HAWKINS: I'm really very happy to see you back

AISHA: Thanks

HAWKINS: Place hasn't been the same without you actually

AISHA: Ah that's nice

HAWKINS: And everything is well?

AISHA: With?

HAWKINS: Generally

AISHA: I guess

HAWKINS: Well that's good

AISHA: Yeah

HAWKINS: Perhaps I could help you with your revision plan?

AISHA: Got that covered thanks

HAWKINS: Right
   You know Aisha, this is an opportunity for a fresh start

AISHA: Cool

HAWKINS: And I believe in you

AISHA: Cool

HAWKINS: And I am here to help you

AISHA: Sure

HAWKINS: …so we don't need to battle each other

AISHA: And why would I think we did?

HAWKINS: Well…good question

AISHA: Sounds like you think that

HAWKINS: No not at all

AISHA: What would Freud say?

Beat.

HAWKINS: Well I suspect he would say I had made an assumption

AISHA: And what would you say?

HAWKINS: I'd be inclined to agree

AISHA smiles.

AISHA: Was that aggressive Miss?

HAWKINS: Do you think it to be?

AISHA: I think it doesn't matter what I think

HAWKINS: Well, I don't think it was

AISHA: I am though aren't I?
Generally. According to the masses

HAWKINS: The masses?

AISHA: Yep

HAWKINS: Powerful women needn't concern themselves with the voice of the masses

AISHA: Nice idea Miss

HAWKINS: Well I'd say it's more / than an…

AISHA: 'Aggressive Aisha and all her aggressivenesssss!' That's right init?

HAWKINS: It's up to you to show people the real you

AISHA: Like find things I'm passionate about and help make a difference in the world?

HAWKINS: Well you know I'm always going to be a fan of that!

AISHA: Like deciding I'm passionate about women's rights

HAWKINS: Well yes...

AISHA: Deciding I'm going to start a feminist group at the college

HAWKINS: We already have one, no?

AISHA: Hypothetically

HAWKINS: Well of course

AISHA: Then deciding we are going to start an online campaign to bring awareness of injustices carried out against women all over the world, like that Miss?

> *No reply.*

Miss?

HAWKINS: That's not technically how it happened / now is...

AISHA: How what happened Miss?

> *Beat.*

HAWKINS: I think, that one must be cautious about how one's passion is displayed

AISHA: Powerful women needn't concern themselves with the voice of the masses

> *HAWKINS looks on.*

Think I should tone myself down Miss?

HAWKINS: Absolutely not what I'm saying

AISHA: Be less concentrated...

HAWKINS: No...

AISHA: More neutral...

HAWKINS: No...

AISHA: ...a nice neutral colour palate...talk about acceptable things like, feminism...the Suffragettes ...yeah...talk about feminism and the Suffragettes because that's an acceptable level of discomfort innit? That what you mean Miss?

HAWKINS: I think you already know the answer to that

AISHA: Reckon that's what the college want

HAWKINS: I'd disagree

AISHA: Reckon that's what society want

HAWKINS: It's a shame you feel that way

AISHA: Nah, it's fuel Miss

HAWKINS: For?

AISHA: Dunno yet

HAWKINS: Perhaps it's important to think of the glass half full instead of half empty

AISHA: Proper optimist innit Miss

HAWKINS: I like to be

AISHA: Rose-tinted glasses and marshmallow clouds…

HAWKINS: If you like

AISHA: You do

HAWKINS: All perspective

AISHA: Lauryn Hill said, 'Fantasy is what they want but reality's what they need'

HAWKINS: Things are a lot better now than they used to be

AISHA: Oh you think so do you?

HAWKINS: I think it is great that you want to make a difference in the world

AISHA: Oh I will

HAWKINS: Great, just try not to let your anger exhaust you however

AISHA: That why I was suspended Miss? Were my words too aggressive, too defensive and angry…

HAWKINS: …Those are certainly not my words Aisha…

AISHA: Is that why I've been home unable to learn, unable to partake. Miss?

HAWKINS: Sometimes we can be hard to read

AISHA: Hard to read like a new language?

HAWKINS: Well, yes if you like

AISHA: Like stepping foot on foreign land and talking to the locals

HAWKINS: Not quite the same thing

AISHA: Like stepping foot on foreign land, talking to the locals…realising you don't understand them so you conquer said locals, rename said land and then change the language of the land, and voilà! Language taken from them

HAWKINS: I think that's an interesting narrative for another time.

AISHA: Miss Aisha!
insert slave master's name here…

HAWKINS: We are more than our names

AISHA: Yet my surname is a reminder of an unnamed Nation, displaced history. 'A people without knowledge of their own history is like a tree without the roots' Marcus Garvey

HAWKINS: There is no doubting that we have seen some horrific days since arriving on this planet

AISHA: Grandad says I can't call myself English

HAWKINS: Okay

AISHA: Born here though

HAWKINS: Well you can call yourself what you like

AISHA: Not English though

HAWKINS: We define ourselves

AISHA: Yeah, I'm not English Miss

HAWKINS: Well my great grandmother was Welsh, and my father's mother is part French

AISHA: Not the same Miss

HAWKINS: Okay

AISHA: No language to call my own, no surname to know from whence I came, a passport that bares a name, that's all

HAWKINS: We musn't define ourselves solely through our history

AISHA smiles.

AISHA: Yeah…

HAWKINS: So would you say you're settling back in okay?

AISHA: I don't know what you want me to say

HAWKINS: Whatever you feel you need to say

AISHA: Yes Miss, everything's great Miss

HAWKINS: You're sure?

AISHA: Drinks machine's moved

HAWKINS: It has?

AISHA: It was on the corner of the biology block

HAWKINS: I hadn't noticed

AISHA: Moved it to the common room now

HAWKINS: Well that's good

AISHA: Already had one there, already had one right by the sliding doors, don't make sense, why change it?

HAWKINS: Perhaps they needed the extra room, I wouldn't like to guess

AISHA: Changed my Media Studies group too, got me sat next to Simple Simon

HAWKINS: Aisha

AISHA: Calls himself that

HAWKINS: Even still

AISHA: Well
   I'm not settled, nothing's settled, won't ever be settled

HAWKINS: What do you think needs to happen for you to settle back in to college life?

AISHA: Dunno

HAWKINS: Well part of the agreement is that we work on a way of re-building relationships within your year group

AISHA: Ain't gonna happen

HAWKINS: It's important that it does

AISHA: I'm not taking down that blog

HAWKINS: Well… Okay…

AISHA: I'm not, I did nothing wrong, you know that

HAWKINS: I think we can both agree that the situation was not dealt with in the best way

AISHA: You can't expel me for writing a blog

HAWKINS: No one said…

AISHA: I was suspended to prove some point…

HAWKINS: …Let's look at solutions rather than problems…

AISHA: …To silence me…

HAWKINS: Moving forward Aisha…

AISHA: Just tell me what I need to do and I'll do it, innit

HAWKINS: Not really how it works

AISHA: So how does it work?

HAWKINS: Well, a little bit of a commitment would be a great start

AISHA: I am committed

HAWKINS: Right

Well, it's about showing it as well as saying it

AISHA: I'm here aren't I?

HAWKINS: And that's a great start, however I'd hope you were also committed to healing the wounds caused amongst the year group

AISHA: Why me?

HAWKINS: Well you are equally responsible

AISHA: Nah this place is

HAWKINS: Aisha, you're far too bright to say things like that

AISHA: It's the truth

HAWKINS: Okay, perhaps we should leave it there

AISHA: These disputes aren't new, my resistance to nodding and smiling are what's new, and that's when it becomes a problem for everyone

HAWKINS: I wouldn't say so, but perhaps this is a conversation best had with Mr Blair

AISHA: Where were the objections when those posters were put up around school? When we were all encouraged to pledge our allegiance to a publication that has dehumanised brown bodies since the beginning of its time

HAWKINS: Aisha some would find your comments inflammatory

   Beat.

AISHA: Fine

HAWKINS: Fine?

AISHA: Yeah

HAWKINS: It's comments like that…

AISHA: Like that?

HAWKINS: Yes…

AISHA: What's that?

HAWKINS: Comments that could be misconstrued

AISHA: Wouldn't want to make people uncomfortable

HAWKINS: Well / exactly…

AISHA: Get my face smashed in

HAWKINS: That's quite a different thing

AISHA: Yeah?

HAWKINS: Extreme

AISHA: World's extreme

HAWKINS: I expected more positivity today Aisha

AISHA: Soz

HAWKINS: Is there something I need to know?

AISHA: Like?

HAWKINS: Anything of concern…

AISHA: Nah Miss

HAWKINS: So why did you… if there is something I need to be made aware of…

AISHA: If there is, you'll do… what?

HAWKINS: Every student should feel safe

AISHA: And if they don't

HAWKINS: You don't?

AISHA: If I didn't

HAWKINS: If you feel like there is a threat to your safety… if you feel like you need to talk

AISHA: In confidence yeah?

HAWKINS: To a point yes

AISHA: Be like therapy yeah?

HAWKINS: No, but if you feel like you need that

AISHA: Therapy?

HAWKINS: Yes

AISHA: Nah I'm good Miss

HAWKINS: It can be a useful avenue when needed

AISHA: You'd like that innit?

HAWKINS: No actually

AISHA: Make you feel good wouldn't it?

HAWKINS: Not at all

AISHA: Help you to sleep better at night knowing you'd helped the apparently failing inner-city youth of today! Eh Miss

HAWKINS: Okay that's enough

AISHA: Now it's enough? Now that you're uncomfortable?

HAWKINS: Look Aisha, your parents really want you to pass your exams

AISHA: No chance of me not

HAWKINS: Well glad to hear it

AISHA: Not that failing troubled teen that needs your saving

HAWKINS: Well good. Part of the commitment to you returning to college is you attending these sessions

AISHA: What's your point?

HAWKINS: I know how hard the last couple of months have been for you, and I know it feels like the world is caving in on you sometimes……

AISHA: Can't walk down the corridor no more Miss, do you understand what I'm saying to you?

HAWKINS: I want to understand

AISHA: Lid's been lifted now Miss… popped off, let the steam out…

HAWKINS: Meaning?

AISHA: Like smoke. Everywhere… world's full of smoke… looks the same… Can't put it back once the lid's popped off Miss

HAWKINS: Aisha I can't help you if you don't open up a little

AISHA: Speak what I mean, mean what I say?

HAWKINS: If it is helpful for you to do so

AISHA: So we can talk about that list you've got me on

>   *Beat.*

HAWKINS: Has there been a specific event since returning to college that has made you feel unsafe?

AISHA: Yeah.

HAWKINS: What happened?

AISHA: A whole load of students were put on some / type of list, a watch list, a spy list…

HAWKINS: Do you feel that this is an appropriate subject matter to be discussing with me Aisha?

AISHA: Do you Miss?

HAWKINS: You said you feel unsafe since returning, let's discuss that

AISHA: Sure

HAWKINS: Has something happened?

AISHA: Yeah I had a blog…

HAWKINS: Aisha…

AISHA: Someone printed a few / entries

HAWKINS: Since you've been back….

AISHA: Said I was inciting hatred / I wasn't

HAWKINS: Aisha, since you have returned to college have you had any events occur I should know about?

AISHA: What difference does it make?

HAWKINS: Again, I can't help you if I don't know

> *No reply.*

Aisha?

AISHA: I like you Miss

HAWKINS: I'm glad

AISHA: You proper care don't you?

HAWKINS: I like to think so

AISHA: You're one of the good ones

HAWKINS: As are you

AISHA: Mum and Dad have been telling me the same thing since I was like seven years old…

HAWKINS: Don't mouth off to teachers?

AISHA: Yeah

HAWKINS: Good

> *Beat.*

AISHA: 'You need to work ten times harder to gain half of their success darling. Don't talk too loud, don't draw attention to yourself. Be the best you can be but don't cause a scene'

> *Bell goes off. AISHA bolts up.*

HAWKINS: Aisha

AISHA: Yeah

HAWKINS: Stay out of trouble

AISHA: 'Course Miss

> *AISHA exits.*

SCENE 5

Rain hammers.

Night.

HAWKINS' flat.

SHABZ: Eat something

HAWKINS: I'm fine

ARCHIE: I can order something

HAWKINS: If you like

ARCHIE: 'If I like'?

HAWKINS: Do I need to feed you and bath you as well Archie?

      Bites his tongue.

SHABZ: All of this will soon blow over you'll see

ARCHIE: Well that's easy for you to say

SHABZ: Not really

ARCHIE: Well

HAWKINS: Stop. Please

      Beat.

ARCHIE: She's told you she's probably suspended

SHABZ: She hasn't been suspended Archie…

ARCHIE: Carry that around with you now won't you

HAWKINS: I have not been suspended

ARCHIE: But it's possible

SHABZ: Have I missed something here?

HAWKINS: No, Archie's just being Archie…

SHABZ: Right, well there's no talk of suspension…

HAWKINS: Thank you

ARCHIE: Do your students turn up at your house then Shabnam?

HAWKINS: For crying out loud…

SHABZ: Not really no

ARCHIE: Ever been asked to take some time off work to… what was it? Gather your thoughts before returning

SHABZ: Pretty standard Archie

ARCHIE: Pretty standard!

SHABZ: Yes, in these circumstances

ARCHIE: But you've never been in one of these circumstances

HAWKINS: ENOUGH

SHABZ: Not sure what your point is

ARCHIE: Nothing's going to simply blow over my love

Awkwardly silent.

Look, you're both clearly still shaken

ARCHIE: Understatement

SHABZ: Okay, but the best thing that you can do is stay / ca…

ARCHIE: People are asking questions, what am I supposed to tell them?

HAWKINS: Whatever you bloody like

ARCHIE: Look, we don't know what that girl is capable of…

HAWKINS: Aisha is… was my student, I know her, I made an informed decision at the time… Or I thought I did

ARCHIE: You made a stupid decision, which has implicated you into an absolute nightmare

SHABZ: We don't know the details

ARCHIE: With all due respect the girl turned up covered in blood

SHABZ: Well let's not jump to conclusions

ARCHIE: It's as plain as day

SHABZ: We simply do not know the details

ARCHIE: We know a boy lost his life

SHABZ: And a girl has pretty much lost hers

ARCHIE: She's alive

SHABZ: But she's lost her life too

ARCHIE: And she deserves to

SHABZ: I'd disagree actually

ARCHIE: Well you would

SHABZ: Meaning?

HAWKINS: Archie what's got into you

ARCHIE: I'm suffocating in here

HAWKINS: Well go out and get some fresh air

ARCHIE: The air's not fresh out there, it's tight, it's tense, no one can predict what will happen when they leave their house, can't breathe out there and I certainly can't breathe in here

    Beat.

HAWKINS: Well I want us to try and calm down

ARCHIE: You opened the door, you brought this in

HAWKINS: And I'd do it again

ARCHIE: This is insane
You're intolerable

SHABZ: Alright, Archie

ARCHIE: With all due respect Shabnam…

SHABZ: Respect? Do you even know the meaning of that word?

HAWKINS: Why are you behaving this way?

ARCHIE: Do you think every lost soul needs saving Shabnam?

SHABZ: What a strange question

ARCHIE: Do you?

HAWKINS: You don't have to answer anything

ARCHIE: I don't see the issue

SHABZ: Well my answer's no

ARCHIE: Interesting

SHABZ: How so?

ARCHIE: Just interesting

HAWKINS: Are you satisfied?

ARCHIE: Partially

SHABZ: Do you?

ARCHIE: Nope, I think people should mind their own business more

SHABZ: Well there you go!

ARCHIE: Well, Sally seems to think it to be her duty to save the world

HAWKINS: That's just not true

SHABZ: We're teachers Archie, we…

ARCHIE: Not just at school

HAWKINS: Where else?

ARCHIE: You carry this guilt around on your shoulders, loud as anything

HAWKINS: Right, so what am I guilty about?

ARCHIE: You tell me

HAWKINS: I have no idea!

ARCHIE: She thinks every lost soul needs saving

SHABZ: Well people save themselves Archie

ARCHIE: Glad to hear it

SHABZ: And I think it's a pretty great thing that Sally has a need to help people

ARCHIE: Well it's expected of us isn't it

SHABZ: Who's us?

HAWKINS: You're out of line Archie

SHABZ: Look, I think it's an unfortunate set of events that Sally's found herself in…

ARCHIE: You've got more of an opinion than that Shabnam

SHABZ: I have opinions on all sorts of things

ARCHIE: Sure

SHABZ: Is there something more specific / you're wanting to ask me?

HAWKINS: No there is not…

ARCHIE: I have all sorts of questions actually

HAWKINS: Great meanwhile I want to get off to bed

SHABZ: I'll let you sleep babe

ARCHIE: Are you a sympathiser?

SHABZ: What?!

HAWKINS: Archie please drop this

SHABZ: Drop what?

HAWKINS: Nothing

SHABZ: Go on

HAWKINS: Nothing Shabnam

ARCHIE: I've been told I can't bring up certain things around you

HAWKINS: I never said that

ARCHIE: Might make you feel uncomfortable

SHABZ: Really?

HAWKINS: It's a misunderstanding

SHABZ: About what?

HAWKINS: Honestly it's nothing

ARCHIE: I felt like it was important that we could have these conversations

HAWKINS: I've already told you, no

ARCHIE: Alright

    Beat.

HAWKINS: We'll catch up tomorrow Shabz

    She hesitates.

SHABZ: What do you mean by sympathiser?

HAWKINS: Look, I think we call it a night now

SHABZ: No

HAWKINS: I categorically do not want to have this conversation in my home tonight

SHABZ: What did you mean?

HAWKINS: God

ARCHIE: Where do your sympathies mostly lie?

HAWKINS: Archie

SHABZ: I don't follow

ARCHIE: Do your sympathies lie with that poor / boy's parents, that heroes parents or…

HAWKINS: Archie stop this now…

ARCHIE: Or the girl?

Beat.

SHABZ: Well I'd imagine the same as you, but I'm guessing that's not the answer you want

ARCHIE: I don't think you're being honest

HAWKINS: It doesn't matter…

ARCHIE: Seems like everyone's allowed an opinion other than me

SHABZ: Oh is that right?!

ARCHIE: In your own backyard, not even a single opinion is allowed to be had

SHABZ: Except this is not your backyard, it's not even your home

ARCHIE: Ah! Well that's the thing. This is my home

Silence.

SHABZ: Are you feeling victimized Archie…

HAWKINS: It's been a long few days and…

SHABZ: …stripped of your right to speak up, or something?

HAWKINS: Shabnam he didn't mean…

SHABZ: I'm asking Archie a question

ARCHIE: Just interested to know where you stand

SHABZ: But that doesn't answer my question now does it

ARCHIE: Yeah, you could say I feel stripped of my right to speak

SHABZ: How does that feel?

ARCHIE: Infuriating

SHABZ: And yet here you are, globally, a walking poster of power

ARCHIE laughs.

ARCHIE: Is that so

SHABZ: You're a man

ARCHIE: Yeah alright

SHABZ: Then there's the other thing

ARCHIE: The other thing?!

SHABZ: Yeah.
So if you feel like you're voiceless, God help the rest of us

Beat.

HAWKINS: I think that's as good a time as any for us to call it a night

SHABZ: Fine

ARCHIE: Now you didn't answer my question, where do you stand?

SHABZ: Right, well right now, in my mate's living room, I stand in my mate's living room, in London in 2016, a year for exposing the beast that lies dormant in the belly of our country, does that answer your question, Archie?

Beat.

ARCHIE: I'd say so

SHABZ: Good

SHABZ gathers her stuff.

I'll give you a call tomorrow Hawks

HAWKINS: Shabz…

SHABZ: Get some sleep

SHABZ leaves

ARCHIE: She'll get you in trouble that one
Thinks the world owes her something

HAWKINS: She does not

ARCHIE: Oh come on

HAWKINS: You've offended one of my dearest friends…

ARCHIE: I could have

HAWKINS: What's got into you?

ARCHIE: Look around you, look at this country
It's falling apart, pulled from underneath us… There
are two-parent families that are surviving on food bank
supplies, working their backsides off and still unable to
make ends meet. People are waiting for weeks on end for
an appointment with their GP, our most needy can't get
a look in on a council property… kids are being raised
here then flying off to train and coming back to bomb the
land, our police can't do their jobs without being accused
of all sorts of insanity, and the whole time the face of this
country the language of this country, the concentration
of this country is changing… And we have no say. We're
supposed to help everyone… Welcome everyone… Gather
all the lost souls and give them a cuddle. That girl is
messed up, and it's not our responsibility to fix her, we owe
her nothing. We don't owe any of them a damn thing

> *Beat.*

HAWKINS: You sound like a…

ARCHIE: …No Sally…

HAWKINS: You sound…

ARCHIE: I resent that

HAWKINS: You do

ARCHIE: And here lies our problem, people speak out and
they're silenced, told we're angry and aggressive

HAWKINS: Yeah

ARCHIE: Everyone else is allowed to speak up, every minority
group has a platform, but we are expected to shut up and
get on

HAWKINS: I'd like to be alone now

ARCHIE: No

HAWKINS: Yes please

ARCHIE: What have I said that is so wrong?

HAWKINS: I can't even dignify that with an answer

ARCHIE: The country we live in today, gives power to that girl allowing her to be seen as a victim of a make believe system that has somehow wronged her and therefore given her license to do what she did to that poor boy

HAWKINS: Good night Archie

ARCHIE: If we can't have these conversations then I don't know…

HAWKINS: You don't know what?

ARCHIE: How can I take care of you if you won't let me

SCENE 6

The cage.

AISHA bangs.

HAWKINS stands on the outside.

AISHA: Let me out I wanna go home!

> *Bangs.*

I said let me out I wanna go home!

> *Bangs.*

I said I wanna go flippin home

HAWKINS: You need to calm down

> *Bangs.*

AISHA: I'm not calming down. Let me out

HAWKINS: Aisha

AISHA: Now

HAWKINS: You need to calm down

AISHA: Place is a joke

HAWKINS: Aisha breathe

AISHA: Receiving extra funds for the vulnerable young, but you marginalise and exploit their needs

> *Bangs.*

HAWKINS: Calm down

AISHA: Hold photo calls, arms wrapped around the token ones, make you look inclusive, make you look progressive. / I want to go home

> *Bangs.*

HAWKINS: I won't talk to you whilst you're like this

> *Bangs.*

AISHA: I don't need you to talk to me. What does talking to you do for me? What has it ever done for me? Can't do nothing for me. You're fraudulent, this whole place is fraudulent.

HAWKINS: Hey! Enough

AISHA: This Great Kingdom of ours!
Strip away our dignity, make us come begging to you for help, make us dependent, take away the needle, take away the smack, dangle it over our heads so we're always in debt. So we always come back

> *Bangs. Bangs. Bangs. Then silence.*

HAWKINS: Your parents are on their way in

AISHA: Don't talk about my parents

HAWKINS: What would they say if they saw you now

AISHA: You know what they'd say

HAWKINS: I want you to think about that

AISHA: I don't care

HAWKINS: You do care

AISHA: Don't tell me what I care about, I told you I don't care, and I don't care

HAWKINS: Alright

AISHA: Good

HAWKINS: I do know that you've worked too hard to throw it all away at this point

AISHA: What difference does it make how hard I've worked? No one don't see me, no one don't recognise my work. When I leave here I'm gonna wear a next mask, play a next game, smile when I wanna smash shit up, smile when I know I'm being discriminated against, keep my voice high pitch, head held high, not too high, make people feel comfortable, pretend I can't see unprecedented fear in their eyes, act like everyday isn't a reminder that my life is of less value than hers every time I step out of my parents' house. Be strong, be unbreakable, smile, don't be intimidating, work hard, work harder. Smile. Ignore. Smile. Smile. Smile. That's what he wanted, and I didn't give it to him

> *Silence.*

HAWKINS: Did you disrupt his class?

AISHA: I challenged him

HAWKINS: Perhaps it's the way in which you went about it that's the problem?

AISHA: Streets are full Miss.

People everywhere. Everyday crowds are gathering in some corner of some English city, asking questions, making noise, demanding to be seen, to be acknowledged. Streets are full Miss. Full with the working class and the English born, the English born with the immigrant face, fighting at the bottom, hating and gutting at each other, killing each other to get a little bit closer to the needle, a little bit closer to the feed. Dying to be seen. Dying to be heard. My Grandfather was invited here by the Queen. For what? For what Miss? What did this place give him? What's it giving me... This! My home... I can't catch my space here.... This, being all I've known, I can't find my space and I'm not supposed to talk about it. I'm not supposed to complain. I'm supposed to blend in, just accept it and I can't.

    Beat.

HAWKINS: I feel awful that you feel this way, I...

AISHA: Are you watching the Olympics Miss?

HAWKINS: When I can

AISHA: I like all the track sports

HAWKINS: Me too

AISHA: Imagine you were a sprinter and you were running drills, and every time you set off you smashed into a pane of glass and fell on your back, you kept getting up and explaining there was a pane of glass there, as real as the earth under your feet, but the entire stadium told you there was no pane of glass. Stop making excuses for yourself! Try again! Work harder! And when you grew frustrated at bruising your body on that pane of glass they told you to calm down, be graceful, don't cause a scene. With every order, every single denial... Another layer gone, another part of you, gone.

HAWKINS: I think... I think there's something in that in which we could all relate to, and it's awful... it's an awful feeling

AISHA: You think you understand but how can you?

You think you understand what it is to be marginalised and held back and somehow through all your apparent empathy for those less fortunate than yourself, you manage to negate any responsibility for your own complicity.

Beat.

HAWKINS: You're so angry

AISHA: I have to be

HAWKINS: It's not good for you. I look at you and I see passion / and intelligence

AISHA: I'm not allowed to be passionate…

HAWKINS: …the world owes you nothing, it was my biggest lesson.

AISHA doesn't respond.

HAWKINS: Aisha…

AISHA: I'm empty

SCENE 7

Daytime.

Rain.

A demonstration.

A loud and bustling street.

CHORUS: We, are gathered here today brothers and sisters, to pay our respects to Officer cadet Joshua Banks.

Crowd cheers.

CHORUS: In an act of sheer evil, brothers and sisters, this brave young man who served his

Queen and country

was taken from us before his time

This small beast of a girl, forced that knife so deep into the flesh of our future. She punctured and punctured until the life drained from behind his eyes and she has shown no remorse. And we seek justice for this crime.

No,

we demand justice for this crime.

We demand that our government start serving the good

honest

loyal

English

people the way in which they were elected to do so.

We are no longer going to sit back and watch our good
country fall apart at the hands of highjackers. The hands of

criminals,

the hands of those that

should not be able to step foot on English soil

Crowd cheers.

I say no more scum clogging our sewers!

Crowd cheers.

CHORUS: No more scum exhausting our NHS and benefit
systems!

No more dirty thieving murderous immigrants clogging
our sewers, grooming our young girls

and erasing our good culture.

It's time to take our country back

Exterminate the cockroaches

Take their children

Teach them discipline

Teach them to respect our people and our land.

They want to illegitimise our argument by calling us

racists

and bigots,

accuse us of

hate crimes

and xenophobia.

But unlike our Liberal brethren I'm not afraid to be seen in a negative light. Unlike our liberals rubbing shoulders with

blacks

and Asians

and Muslims

and terrorist sympathizers,

though they secretly fear them.

I will not smile in their face and clutch my bag as they pass me in the street. I say I'm not scared to be called those things, I welcome those labels, I encourage those labels

Come to my face and

call me a racist,

come to my face and call me a bigot and I will show you a woman, a wife, a mother, a leader a good citizen that loves her country, that will die for her country, that wishes to see no harm caused to no human being. But I will fight, I will draw blood, I will take my last breath before I let this government allow these intruders to kill the spirit of my Kingdom.

This is our Land

We will defend the honour of our heroes by any means necessary

Crowd cheer.

CHORUS: Call the guards
Raise the flags
Release the hounds
Draw your guns
Protect your Land
Stand your Ground
Show no fear
We ain't moving
We ain't scared.

Call the guards
Raise the flags
Release the hounds
Draw your guns
Protect your land
Protect your land
Stand your ground
This is war
This is what we're fighting for.
Gas them all
Crush them all
Beat them 'til they learn the rules
Kill their kids
Burn their kids
Beat them 'til they remember this.
Protect my land. Protect the land. Protect our land
Send 'em back
Send them where their bodies rot
Call the guards
Raise the flags
The slaves are planning to attack
Draw your guns
Call the guards
Release the hounds
Protect the land

SCENE 8

Rain.

Lunchtime.

HAWKINS' living room – The room is turned upside down.

SHABZ: You look like shit

HAWKINS: Thanks

SHABZ: …And your house smells like stale B.O. Don't look at me for sympathy until you've brushed your teeth

HAWKINS: Honestly, I'm not…

SHABZ: In the mood. Neither am I

HAWKINS: Shabz, I can't face anyone right now

SHABZ: Ah, is that why you haven't returned any of my calls

HAWKINS: I just needed some peace

SHABZ: Well that I can accept

HAWKINS: Great

SHABZ: As long as that's the real reason
How's Archie?

HAWKINS: I wouldn't know

SHABZ: You haven't seen him?

HAWKINS: No

SHABZ: Alright! Can I ask when your meeting is?

HAWKINS: I can't remember, can't think about that right now

SHABZ: I need you back

> *Beat.*

Barbara's flirting with the caretaker again

> *Laughs.*

HAWKINS: She's not?

SHABZ: Asked him out to the bingo last I heard

HAWKINS: Fuck off!

SHABZ: It'll all kicking off! You're missing out

> *She laughs herself into tears.*

Are you crying?

HAWKINS: No

SHABZ: Yeah you are

HAWKINS: A bit

SHABZ: Well I don't know what you'd want me to do with those tears

HAWKINS: Oh fuck off Shabz

SHABZ: You're allowed five minutes of feeling sorry for yourself, and then you need to get up and be counted

HAWKINS: Steller advice

SHABZ: I'm serious

HAWKINS: Yeah I get it thanks

SHABZ: It's awful, all of it. But there is a young girl locked up in a prison accused of murdering a boy that the press are naming a local hero and you're crying? Honestly…. what…what am I supposed to say

HAWKINS: Why are you here?

SHABZ: Because you won't answer my calls and someone had to check in on you, and I'll be damned if it's just Archie

HAWKINS: Right, well I already feel like shit

SHABZ: Do you even know why?

HAWKINS: What…yes I know why…what's your problem?

SHABZ: I don't have one

HAWKINS: You know, I'm sick of you and you're 'oh she can't possibly understand' shit!

SHABZ: Do I say that to you?

HAWKINS: Seriously….

SHABZ: Have I ever said that to you?

HAWKINS: I'm allowed to feel shit

SHABZ: That you are

HAWKINS: I don't need to have walked a mile in your shoes to feel shit about something that has happened to me

SHABZ: Happened to you?

HAWKINS: Yes me!

SHABZ: Must be awful

HAWKINS: It is

SHABZ: …all of these things that are happening to you in your kited out flat, in the corner of this quiet little cul-de-sac and your hip little bakery down the street

HAWKINS: You've walked in here and you've judged me

> *Beat.*

SHABZ: No

HAWKINS: Yeah you have

SHABZ: Your flat stinks yeah

HAWKINS: Don't joke, we're not doing that

SHABZ: It's about what you don't do

HAWKINS: Like what?

SHABZ: Like…Listen I'm not here to shit on you

HAWKINS: Well that's nice

SHABZ: I mean it, but…

HAWKINS: What?

SHABZ: We've never fallen out, that's rare

HAWKINS: What's your point?

SHABZ: That night, with Archie

HAWKINS: It was a shit night and I asked you both to stop numerous times

SHABZ: Some of the things he was implying…

HAWKINS: That was him not me

SHABZ: But he feels those things

HAWKINS: He was bang out of order doesn't matter anyway, we're not together anymore

SHABZ: Right

HAWKINS: And I don't want to talk about it

SHABZ: Okay. Well I hope you're alright

HAWKINS: I'm fine

SHABZ: And I hope all of this has helped to open your eyes a little bit

HAWKINS: To what?

SHABZ: Well things maybe you don't ordinarily notice

HAWKINS: Like?

SHABZ: You're silent. You're always silent when you should speak up

HAWKINS: Bollocks

SHABZ: He took your voice, you gave him your voice

HAWKINS: No I never

SHABZ: Yeah, you did

HAWKINS: Look if I needed relationship advice from Miss serial singleton then I'd ask

SHABZ: I'm right though, you know it.

HAWKINS: If you say so

SHABZ: The things he said to me…

HAWKINS: He knows he was wrong

SHABZ: Does he

HAWKINS: Yes

SHABZ: It's not about condemning him, it's about recognising that he felt comfortable enough to say those things to me in front of you.

HAWKINS: I asked him to stop

SHABZ: You act like you don't see things, but you do. Archie, Aisha… You knew her behaviour was becoming more worrying, you told me yourself that you thought that she shouldn't have been expelled

HAWKINS: Well I couldn't have done anything about that

SHABZ: Really?

HAWKINS: They didn't think her blog and the things she was posting were acceptable…I mean I saw some of them

SHABZ: It's not really about the blog

HAWKINS: Enlighten me then, because you're treating me like I'm stupid

SHABZ: You let them take that girl's voice away from her, she wrote about her experiences, as a young woman having been born into a country that she does not feel safe in, and it made you uncomfortable

HAWKINS: Yeah it fuckin made me uncomfortable, it was a divisive, quite confrontational blog and it interfered with relations at the college

SHABZ: So you reported her?

HAWKINS: How dare you

SHABZ: I'm just asking

HAWKINS: I don't need to answer that.

SHABZ: Fair enough

HAWKINS: In fact I think you should leave

SHABZ: Perhaps I should, because if it's a problem for someone like her

HAWKINS: Like her?

SHABZ: Like me

HAWKINS: Have I missed something here?

SHABZ: Probably…

HAWKINS: You are bang out of line

SHABZ: Am I?

HAWKINS: We don't do this… this is not our story

SHABZ: Because we're the same, because the world treats us the same

HAWKINS: I didn't say that

SHABZ: Nobody that has experienced what Aisha has experienced has anytime for guilty tears.

HAWKINS: Okay, yeah you should leave

SHABZ: Fine

HAWKINS: And next time you want to reduce our friendship to race / give me a heads up

SHABZ: Is that what you think this is? Is that what you think this is?

HAWKINS: Yes! You're telling me what a horrible human being I am because I… what? Didn't grow up with the same issues you did, because all of you obviously had the same experiences

> *Beat.*

SHABZ: Do you see how easy it is for you to become the victim?

HAWKINS: Yes, because you're being accusatory

SHABZ: I'm not

HAWKINS: Yeah, you are

SHABZ: You're my friend…

HAWKINS: You sure about that?

SHABZ: You're my friend and I have adored you since we did our placement. We've gone through everything together

HAWKINS: Then why are you behaving like you don't know my / heart?

SHABZ: Let me finish, because I love you

HAWKINS: Of course you do

SHABZ: My other friends don't love you though, my boyfriends have never loved you, my Mum…

HAWKINS: What do I say to that?

> *Beat.*

SHABZ: I love you despite of the things you're unaware of, I love you even though you like to wear bindis as a fashion accessory and let your prick of boyfriend black up for Halloween…

HAWKINS: Shabz that was ages ago…and I spoke to him about that…

SHABZ: …and I love you despite the fact that when you first met my brother and you didn't know he was my brother you were scared

HAWKINS: That's not true

SHABZ: You were

> I love you even though when we go to a teachers' conference and we're stuck talking to snobby old farts you pretend not to notice that the other heads of years direct their conversation to you, instead of me, their peer. I love you even though you pretend not to see it

> *Beat.*

HAWKINS: So what? You've come here to call me a ra…a what? Why? Why did you come here?

SHABZ: Because, I love you enough to say that I think…
You're the problem, not Archie

Silence.

HAWKINS: Well, it's good to know what you think of me

SHABZ: Don't do that

HAWKINS: No really, you think I'm what? You think I've had some magical life, grown up with a silver spoon in my mouth, don't know what it's like to be discriminated against…

SHABZ: Never said that…

HAWKINS: How little to you think of me?

SHABZ: I think you're a good person

HAWKINS: Evidently not

SHABZ: If you listened to what I said

HAWKINS: I don't want to listen to anymore

SHABZ: Hawks…

HAWKINS: I didn't ask for my life, that… That you evidently think has been perfect

SHABZ: I didn't say that

HAWKINS: I'm a good person and I care about people and you… You obviously don't know me like I thought you did

SHABZ: I don't know how you can take that from what I've just said to you?

HAWKINS: Do you know what, get out

SHABZ: What?!

HAWKINS: Yes, get out

Beat.

SHABZ: See those nut jobs out there, flying their St George with their pitbulls and mean mugging, I respect them, they know who they are and they know what they believe in, you see the flames and you know not to put your hand in. But people like you, with your ideals and your moral high grounds, Give to charity during Children in Need, fill out those change.org petitions for those horrible leaders from those horrible countries. Keep your token friend around to feel good about yourself... People like you, well you're a bit harder to make out through the mist.

SHABNAM walks round HAWKINS and leaves. HAWKINS sobs.

SCENE 9

Rain hammers down.

London's burning.

Chorus emerge.

AISHA, unlike before.

Crowd cheer.

A protest grows in numbers.

CHORUS: How many more parents will send their children to school to be spied on and wrongfully accused of crimes?

CHORUS: No justice! No peace!

CHORUS: How many more parents will put their faith in our education system?

CHORUS: How many more students will be detained without charges? It could be any of us! It will be any of us

CHORUS: No justice! No peace!

CHORUS: Streets ain't safe! Can't find no place to escape

CHORUS: No justice! No peace!

CHORUS: This is for every young boy that has been stopped and searched for no good damn reason

CHORUS: No justice! No peace!

CHORUS: This is for all of us, living in a country not designed for us!

CHORUS: No justice! No peace!

CHORUS: This is for every single one of us that wants an equal society for our children and our children's children!

CHORUS: No justice! No peace!

CHORUS: No justice no peace! No justice no peace! No justice no peace!

AISHA: THIS IS OUR ENGLAND!

The crowd cheer.

Red white and the blue!
Today it will see me!
Today it will know me!
Today it will feel me!
This is our England!
Built on the backs of his ancestors on the backs of her ancestors.
On the backs of my ancestors hands laced with blood
An island built on the backs of those you have conquered
An island rich from those you have stolen and forgotten
This is our England!
Out of your sewers I have risen
I, dark wanderer you shield your fair maiden sons from
Veiled monster praying in her mosque
Crippled nomad you have banished to the backs of your caves
We stand before you here today.
Erased from our textbooks, banished to your sidelines,
relegated to your kitchens your toilets, don't gasp or try
to deny this. Comfort in my demise; No more will I sit in
silence whilst you kill our history and crush our dreams.
We come for our reparations.

All that you stole from our souls. I will return to my throne. I will return to my throne
For we come from ancient Kingdoms. Born of Kings and Queens from Kings and Queens, not slaves nor apes, or over sexualised bate.
This is Our England.
Land of the mighty land of great decree
Land of the monarch where our Queen eats for free.
THIS is our England
Land promised to we
'come home your Mother needs your services in blissful harmony we will be'
This is our England
Where we shoot up their country hold illegal wars in their countries judge and jury without a single doubt. We will replace your fear with the love from our hearts.
And we will rise up together, watch your Kingdom Fall. We will march 'til they hear us, we will shout 'til they free us, we will occupy 'til they cease to deny us.
Today they will know us by our names. Today they will call us by our names. Today they will see me wild blood pumping fast through my veins
Today they'll hear me shout
Today they'll hear me chant
This is our England.
This is our England.
This is our England.
Of that there is no doubt!

The city burns. The people remain…

ALWAYS ORANGE

This world to me is as a lasting storm, Whirring me from my friends.

Pericles Act IV, sc I

In addition to all the acting, literary and creative personnel
listed the author would like to thank the following:
Jan Connor, David Ford (translation), Ciaran Grace, Lewis
Grace, Esther Green, Grace Kempster OBE, the Malta Writers
group, Joe Phillips and Andrea Porter.

This play is dedicated to the Green family, of Walthamstow.

Characters

JOE – a British man

NO NAME – a young British male

RUSHA – a British woman

NIALL – a British male, teenage

DOLORES – an American women

AMNA – a young N. African woman

HOUIDA – Amna's friend

FAROUK – a North African man

Jackie, Lorna, Shermeera, Parvendra, Mr Ibrahim,
& No Name II are played by members of the cast.

The British characters should be cast to reflect the multiracial
city in which they live.

Notes on Performance:

Prologue and *To Infinity…* apart, the order of scenes is open, but all the scenes must be used. Likewise, the titles of scenes may be given in production, or not.

Theatrical methods should be used to deliver the noise of explosions where possible, particularly at the outset, but may progress toward more naturalistic sound effects.

Speech given in parenthesis, following ellipsis…(indicates where the line is going). As much of this may be spoken as required before the speaker is interrupted by another speaker, or by a new thought of the speaker's own. If there is no speech in parenthesis following the dots, either the implication is clear, or the speaker is unable or unwilling to follow where the thought is leading.

The quote from Henry James is taken from *The Ambassadors*, Wordsworth Classic edition 1992, p258

The Joni Mitchell lyric is from her song, *A Case of You*, from the album *Blue* © 1970, Joni Mitchell

.

PROLOGUE

The speaker, JOE, wears a business suit, tattered and scorched. He may have prompt notes, questions he has prepared for himself to answer.

Why bother listening to
so many fine words –

How Our Beloved City Fell;
Who lives in cities anymore?
You don't.
Cities are…

What can we gain from dwelling in the past?
We dwell in tents, now, mostly.
You've seen the kind;
Back when we had television sets, air conditioning
smart phones and confidence, we saw
tents like these all the time. They
may have been called shelters.
Now it's us who need them.
Well. That's different.

Why tell how a city was lost when
there is no longer a city to save?
The point of a cautionary tale is
to stop others dead – Yes?
Frozen in tracks made
by your own feet.

Why talk about a home we have no chance of returning to,
ever?
Honestly?
It's relaxing.
You try making a future, try clearing the smallest space
when the universe is rubble – that's hard work. Exhausting.
Why *not* think about old times,
the old city?

Think about trees, think how
every part of the city you loved
slotted together

one organism.
Think how every group
moved around each other, tore strips off each other,
used each other,
stood off each other, mostly;
saw every other collection of people as
quaintly or stupidly other.

Defeating the other
– that felt good.
A sale, a contract,
a football match –
Win then? Win-win;
double measure of pleasure.
Big smile.
Yes!

Everyone knew what that meant, oh yes.
We are the best, we are a clever fucking people –
top dog around this place.

Contacts are useful, obviously:
someone helps you, you help him,
his sister is kind to your mother sometime:
East side people are all right.
What? I'll never trust an East-sider
O come on, you've got to admit
there's good and bad on every side
There's bad in you, for a start.
I suppose.

That's how a city works;
We know who we are, surrounded
by people we are not.
A West-sider sets himself up as a banker – that's expected;
West-siders can always turn a profit.
South-siders? Programming.
Terminal people – those Neanderthals that live by the station –
Construction. Seriously
don't mess around with those people
they are very likely to kill you.

That little girl
that central zone girl, you know the one
she grew up.
sways down the road every morning under your balcony
stilletos, dangled from one finger.
Dear God
which of our women ever rolled her hips like that?

Think about those times.
Times you wanted to know better what
you knew you didn't know the
first thing about, just
out of curiosity.
Tantalised. Teased by otherness,
by the other.

In the months it took for our city to be destroyed
it dawned on those of us who didn't die,
we pushed the wrong boundary.
Love is no longer the universal emotion.
We value fear more than anything.
May everyone everywhere wake tomorrow in the coldest of
sweats:
Maybe they won't dare come down here,
steal our shelters.

In a living city, walls are walls
a post code is a postcode
but this place…

We have found
there is no belonging
no zone of danger, no safe place
in rubble, there is only
familiarity
which I suppose is the beginning
of something.

Where is this boundary, the one we should have known
better than to push at?
Honestly?

It's here

Pause.

Look out
be wary
there are monsters here
Seriously?
That would explain it.

Listen to the history of a city that
That used to argue over cycle lanes
And the glories of cold brew coffee
and now is ash

Lights.

JACKIE'S LAST DAY

A busy office.

JOE: Okay everyone can you all just – can you just pause for a
   moment.
   Thanks. Thank you. So, er…
   I think you all know this is a big week for the company.
   NOT because we signed a new contract…

>   *Cheers*

   It's important because
   Unbelievably
   This is Jackie's last week with us
   where is Jackie?
   Jackie everyone.

>   *Applause as people turn to face a self-conscious JACKIE.*

   Come on Jackie, face your public…

>   *NO NAME has entered, carrying a backpack, or gripping a bag
>   across his/her chest. Walks centre stage, stealing attention.*

NO NAME: Listen to me. EVERYONE.

>   *Beat.*

JOE: Sorry can I help you?

NO NAME: I'm downstairs.

JOE: I'm sorry?

NO NAME: I'm downstairs. In the…
   the thing.

JOE: The thing.

NO NAME: I don't know what you call it. The
   place under this place

JOE: You're in the carpark?

NO NAME: Close.

JOE: Foyer? Reception.

> If you want
> Tyson Workfair Palmer keep going up
> one more floor.

NO NAME: More glass, all…
>   So much glass in this place

JOE: Oh, I see, sorry. You're down there,
>   in the atrium.

NO NAME: Atrium. That's it. I've
>   got there. I
>   reached it.

>> *Beat.*

JOE: Right. So er…we were just…

NO NAME: Sure, I'll just wait.

JOE: Fine. Thankyou.

>   So, as I was saying… (this is Jackie's last week with us.)

>> *JOE is interrupted.*

NO NAME: Atrium – nice word.
>   Glass all the way up:
>   – takes your
>   breath away.

>> *Beat.*

JOE: Yes. It's an impressive building.

NO NAME: I've not been in here – down here – before.
>   in a place like this –
>   what do they call it?
>   The Beer Glass –
>   Ever. I'm thinking
>   How come I live a
>   stone's throw from here
>   I've never been in?

>> *Beat. Tolerant smile. JOE clears his throat again, continues.*

JOE: As co-regional director they said would I say a few words
and of course I said
I'll be delighted. What they didn't know, they'd forgotten
probably, is
when I started with the company, fifteen years ago, Jackie
was…
(already in post, sorting out the world.)

NO NAME: Must be all the glass.
Makes it so light
blinding, almost.
That's what I have to be now
glass
I keep that thought, right here.

> *Beat.*

JOE: Sorry, I don't want to be rude, but we're trying…

NO NAME: People look through me now, that's
a good thing.
Right?

> *Beat.*

JOE: I suppose.

NO NAME: Be glass. Be ice.

> *Beat.*

JOE: Do you want to sit down? Can we get him…(a chair, or a
drink?)

NO NAME: I'll stand. Thanks.
I'll do one shall I?
Ask a question:
'Don't be kind
to your enemy'.

JOE: Actually that's not a…(…question)

> *Beat.*

JOE: Where did you pop up from, actually? What's your name?

NO NAME: No name. I said, I'm not
　　here. Not
　　right here. Please
　　carry on.

JOE: It's just we need to…

NO NAME: Go on. Say your words.
　　Make your speech.

　　　Beat.

JOE: Your bag looks heavy.
　　Is it?

NO NAME: Should be. Ton of
　　nails, scrap metal, old screws,
　　a photo of my brother

JOE: Your brother? Do I know him?

NO NAME: My brother was martyred for the…thing.

JOE: You're on some kind of protest, are you?

NO NAME: Protest?
　　we don't do protests. That would be…(ridiculous)
　　I'm here for the caliphate.
　　Do you begin to get why this –
　　– everything, here –
　　is an offence to god?
　　My brother was martyred for the future.

　　　Pause.

NO NAME: A window must be open somewhere
　　Words rattle about
　　I hear someone say something about fifteen beers…
　　my throat's rasping, I know it's haraam but seriously
　　I could kill a beer
　　honest to god…

JOE: Fifteen years ago – When I
　　started
　　Fifteen years

Not beers

NO NAME: I only caught snatches.
　　　Chill, man.

　　　　　Beat.

JOE: It's fine.

NO NAME: Sounded like beers.

　　　　　Beat.

JOE: Fifteen years ago, when I started with the company
　　　Our friend Jackie
　　　was already in post.

　　　　　Beat.

　　　She'd lost a child, not long before.
　　　Anthony.
　　　Consequently
　　　she'd spent some time in the Greek Islands
　　　Seeing if they could recover
　　　Seeing if Robin, her husband and her
　　　Could salvage something
　　　anything
　　　From their life together.
　　　The answer saddened them both.
　　　And then she started here,
　　　Jackie brought order to what had been
　　　in the early days, I'm told
　　　a very chaotic office.
　　　She was even then
　　　magnificent.

NO NAME: Chaos? in this place?

JOE: We had a Nissen hut back then
　　　by the airport.

NO NAME: You got in early, then.

JOE: Employee Seventeen.

NO NAME: In at the beginning.

JOE: As I said, Employee Seventeen.

NO NAME: She must have been what – twelve?
Number ten?

>*Beat.*

JOE: Admin got cheques, not numbers
There wasn't much cash around
Creatives got paid in pizza and shares
mostly.

NO NAME: Loaded now then.

>*Beat.*

JOE: Who would have guessed, that one day
All these years on, long after we'd stopped working together
we'd be in the same place
Jackie and me
the day everything was ripped apart.
Physically.

NO NAME: Ten elephants, nine elephants, eight…

>*Continues over/under the following.*

JOE: pulled together
especially for the moment.
I was unhurt, practically,
barely a scratch, but Jackie
she retreated, once I began
not one for attention
I sensed her, off to my right
by the window
Sorry Joe, can I interrupt,
she says,
Something's going on downstairs,
in the atrium

NO NAME: Stand back! All of you.

JOE: I held Jackie's scalp in my hand for maybe thirty minutes.
And then I realised what it was.

Beat.

NO NAME: I never saw glass like this in my life
A whole city poured into one stab of light.
In the quiet after I shouted
I wanted to say, to shout so it rang round the whole place
Hey, Employee Seventeen
If you're listening
guess what?

JOE: don't talk to me
don't speak
you unspeakable piece of shit.

NO NAME: Close.
I'm a mist now
smeared on the wall
Sprayed on people's glasses
We are like the grains of sand on the seashore.
That's what our teacher says
I never liked teachers at school but
this guy, he's a prophet, right?
Come to us from the future.
Guess what?
I'm his messenger.
Raise the flag.
RAISE THE FLAG
Bang.

A moment. The bomb explodes.

Lights.

RUSHA'S LAST DAY

A school bell emerges from the chaos of the previous scene, heard off. Also, offstage, a football chant.

RUSHA is waiting for her class to arrive, a pile of completed marking in her arms.

RUSHA: Okay form up over there.

(*Calling.*) Quiet, Niall!!

That side of the room okay.

SHERMEERA: Can't we sit down a bit?

NIALL: Where's the rest Miss?

RUSHA: Bognor Regis. Geography trumps Spanish, apparently.

SHERMEERA: Miss, I'm tired…

RUSHA: Sitting is for wimps, alright.

LORNA: Miss, you can't say that…!

RUSHA: I can today Lorna, okay. Different lesson.

RUSHA: No Samir?

PARVENDRA: Work placement, leisure centre.

NIALL: Pissed out of his head.

SHERMEERA: Drowning in the pool, I hope.

RUSHA flops the files onto the floor.

RUSHA: Okay couple of you spread these out for me – Niall, Parvendra.

LORNA: What do we have to do miss?

RUSHA: Spread them out, so
there's space between them
Come on Shermeera you've got bags of ability
I'm sure you can shuffle a few exam papers.
Alright, so you've all had your results
Some are good well done

Some are not so good

NIALL: Some are shit miss

RUSHA: Some are shit – and where does shit work come from?

PUPILS: *(Chorus.)* Arseholes.

RUSHA: Easy to be an arsehole, agreed Niall?

NIALL: Yes miss.

RUSHA: Easy as filling your pants,
　　　Which is what we do when we're three years old
　　　Not when we're an adult.

NIALL: Hey, Miss thinks I'm an adult.

SHERMEERA: My brother fills his pants:

　　　Special needs – you think I'm joking?

PARVENDRA: Bit prejudiced Miss.

RUSHA: Okay – all over that side.
　　　When I say go, cross the room
　　　Get to the otherside
　　　Only tread on the exam papers. Goddit?
　　　Go
　　　GO
　　　No feet anywhere but on the papers
　　　That's good – excellent.
　　　You see, all that learning helps.

　　　　　They have crossed the room.

RUSHA: Good.
　　　Except – it's over.

　　　　　Beat.

PARVENDRA: What's over?

RUSHA: Modern languages are no longer to be a facet of this
　　　academy. There. Official.

LORNA: Come again Miss?

　　　　　RUSHA begins to pick up some of the exam papers.

89

RUSHA: Languages are educational extras, Lorna.
　　No cash for
　　peripheral activities.
　　So today's lesson is all about what happens when
　　more and more is taken away.

　　　　She has cleared away several papers.

　　Okay, so – try again.
　　all of you – go on
　　Cross the room, just on the papers
　　GO!!
　　Do your best.

NIALL: Cubs, do your best!

　　　　They cross the room.

RUSHA: See – the odds are against us now.
　　The Leisure centre will be requisitioned soon,
　　to house flood victims…

SHERMEERA: You reckon there's going to be a flood miss?

NIALL: Global warming, twat.

RUSHA: …Or it'll be used to house asylum seekers
　　victims of wars
　　we're fighting with half the middle east

PARVENDRA: I'm not fighting no war.

LORNA: Me neither.

SHERMEERA: You think I am?

RUSHA: Or just to give shelter to migrants, wanting a better life.
　　That's a flood too
　　apparently.
　　What better time to scrap languages?
　　Who needs to talk to the neighbours?!

NIALL: It's not the Spanish moving in round us, Miss.

RUSHA: Oh great, Niall. So,
　　Find an exam paper you trod on last time

He finds one.

RUSHA: Who's is it?

NIALL: Shermeera's.

RUSHA: Rip it up.

Beat.

SHERMEERA: Miss I need mine
I have to show it to my dad

RUSHA takes the exam paper.

RUSHA: Honestly?
Counts for nothing
Everyone

Pick up an exam paper.

Got one?
Rip it up.

Beat.

LORNA: Miss, are you having a mental breakdown?

RUSHA: Like this.

She rips it up. They follow suit.

RUSHA: Throw it in the air.

SHERMEERA: I'm fetching Mr Ibrahim

RUSHA: Shermeera come back. Shermeera… (I'm still speaking.)

SHERMEERA exits.

RUSHA: Appealing to authority figures.
That'll help.

Try getting across now.
Shit, isn't it.
And shit is for…?

PUPILS: Arseholes

RUSHA: And we are arseholes – why?

PARVENDRA: We put up with intolerable things.

RUSHA: We put up with stupid,
stupid decisions like this.
Who needs more than one language?
English
steamrollers the globe
– flattens everything
– never mind the culture we miss out on

Art, science

Precious histories
we can't access
stories that get lost,
stories telling people where they're from, who they are,
why they belong

Why they matter, in fact…

> *A knock on the door. Enter MR IBRAHIM.*

RUSHA: Mr Ibrahim. Nice suit.

IBRAHIM: Miss Murthy
A word please.

RUSHA: Sorry, I can only get it down to two words for you just
now Mr Ibrahim.
The second word is off.

> *Beat.*

RUSHA: We could do it in Spanish.

IBRAHIM: My office. Now.

RUSHA: Lorna – My office? Now?

LORNA: *Mi oficina. ¡Ahora!*

RUSHA: Excellent, well done Lorna.

IBRAHIM: Very good, Lorna.
(To RUSHA.) I imagine you think this is clever.

RUSHA: Niall?

NIALL: *Itso te parece gracioca?*

RUSHA: Fantastic, or you could say '*Imagino que te cées lista.*'

IBRAHIM: I'm trying to help you Miss Murthy, you're not helping anyone.

PARVENDRA: *Estoy tratardo de ayudarte, Senora Murthy, no ayudes a nadie así?*

RUSHA: Not bad, Parvendra. *Bueno!*

> *MR IBRAHIM is now very emphatic.*

IBRAHIM: Miss Murthy. *Mi oficina, AHORA.*

> *Beat.*

NOW.

> *MR IBRAHIM exits.*

RUSHA: Oops.

PARVENDRA: Is it true Miss

RUSHA: Is what true, Parvy?

PARVENDRA: If you leave the college
we can drop languages?

> *Pause.*

> *RUSHA exits. The pupils stand bewildered.*

LORNA: What was that?
Seriously?

PARVENDRA: Fuck knows

NIALL: Fucking self-destruct woman
Hey – Parvy – Raise the Flag!

PARVENDRA: I am not a jihadi!
I'm not even a fucking mos…(lem)

> *They freeze; they have heard something.*

LORNA: What was that?
Did you feel that?!

Parvendra looks out of a high window.

PARVENDRA: There.

NIALL: What is that?

PARVENDRA: God knows.

> *LORNA checks her phone.*

LORNA: Nothing.

NIALL: Refresh. Refresh!!

LORNA: Piss off dickhead.

> *The gather around and wait. LORNA reads from her phone.*

LORNA: Explosion, east side…

> *Pause – they are still waiting.*

LORNA: … Beer Glass. What's the Beer Glass?

> *They react to another explosion.*

NIALL: Christ!

PARVENDRA: Don't move. Nobody move!

> *RUSHA enters, and stands with them. Everyone's attention is fixed on something we can't see.*
>
> *Lights.*

FRIENDS IN THE NORTH

A room in a student hostel in North Africa.

A bed. Books. AMNA is onstage, wearing a hijab in the college colour. She is packing books into her college bag, and talking to HOUIDA who is offstage.

AMNA: Move yourself, won't you?
  We have Mr Farouk first thing.
  Then Arabic. Did you do your Arabic, Houida?

> *HOUIDA appears, doing a crazy dance. She is wearing a pillowcase over her head.*

HOUIDA: How do I look?

> *AMNA sees her and laughs.*

AMNA: What are you doing? Idiot! We're going to be late now.

> *HOUIDA pulls off the pillowcase with a flourish. Underneath, her own hijab is in place. She gives us a twirl.*

HOUIDA: De-dah! I'm ready – you see, underneath I am still a
  modest woman.

AMNA: You're crazy.
  How's mine?

HOUIDA: Good, Amna. Professional.

> *Beat.*

Let's sit for a while, there's no rush, not really.

AMNA: We have five minutes – not that.

HOUIDA: I won't be here to sit with tomorrow.

> *Beat.*

AMNA: Your cousin should get someone else. She has sisters,
  doesn't she?

HOUIDA: I promised, it's just a few days.

> *HOUIDA flops onto the bed, lying on her back.*

95

> *A moment.*

HOUIDA: If it was up to me, I'd never leave this room, ever.

> *AMNA joins her on the bed – they are lying side by side. Maybe they hold hands.*

AMNA: How would we study, if we did stay here?

HOUIDA: You don't need to. You have brains enough. Brains and brains.
All I want is to live a life of quiet faithfulness.
You could live it too.
We could mess about all the time.

> *She tickles AMNA, or slaps her with a pillow – the two of them shrieking with laughter.*

AMNA: Stop it!

HOUIDA: *(Mock serious.)* You know, a Moslem is a lover of peace.
Surrender your anger!
Come on we have to go.

AMNA: Oh, now you want to go.

HOUIDA: Yes. I can't wait to show my modest face to the world.

AMNA: I noticed.

> *They adjust each other's hijabs.*

AMNA: Yes?

HOUIDA: Yes, yes. Run to Farouk. Go go go!!

> *They exit. Lights.*

SCARED SHITLESS

DOLORES and JOE. A non-descript office space. There are no chairs. DOLORES carries an iPad. She has swiped her way in, sees the room.

DOLORES: Can't offer you a seat I'm afraid.

> *She goes to raise the blind.*

Great concept, hot-desking
don't you think?

JOE:

DOLORES: Why don't we start over. With everything.
Anything you recall.

JOE: Fine.
I've not had a very eventful life.

DOLORES:

JOE: Hard to know, what might be useful.

DOLORES: Impossible.
So, in your own time. Anything you remember, from the Beer
Glass.

JOE: I remember waking up.
It was … eery.
How many floors are we now?

DOLORES: Third floor.

JOE: I was disoriented.
People used to say disorientated
More syllables. Less of a rush…
I wasn't out long. I think.

> *That's it – there's nothing else he remembers.*

DOLORES: But this was post the event itself,
when you woke

JOE: I don't sleep in the office normally, if that's an issue.

DOLORES: I'm just trying to be thorough.

JOE: Good. Excellent.

    Pause.

DOLORES: So you came around, following the blast…

JOE: I came round, yes, I woke up
   my feet were cold
   My clothes were shredded, but
   it was my feet I noticed.
   There was glass, everywhere.
   For some reason I was afraid of
   bleeding,
   bleeding and not stopping.

    Beat.

DOLORES: You're not a haemophiliac.
   Are you?

JOE: I couldn't work out what would stop it,
   the blood,
   of the city – that's ridiculous.
   There was no one left to stop anything
   I felt as though it was no longer possible to stop
   all this
   stuff
   pouring out of me. Of us. To
   staunch it, staunch the flow.
   Once it started, it would go on.
   Jackie – Mrs Tremarco – she was a trained nurse
   I remembered thinking that.
   Then I remembered she wasn't
   with us anymore.

DOLORES: With the company?

JOE:

JOE: She's one of the names on your list.

    DOLORES consults the iPad.

DOLORES: Tremarco.

JOE: She was standing by the window

DOLORES: By the atrium

JOE: the full force of whatever happened
    happened to Jackie.
    She took the blow for us.

     Beat.

DOLORES: So that's good, Joe: helpful
    you remember something from
    before the blast.
    Mrs Tremarco, by the window.

JOE: Could be a painting
    Mrs Tremarco, by the window;
    Vermeer, maybe.
    The split second before...
    He's good at that
    Vermeer
    When I see a portrait now
    in a frame, some merchant smiling out
    I think
    Bloody idiot – any minute now.

     Beat.

It was her last day
Did you know?
Sorry. I'm not sure I see the point in this,
I hardly remember anything.

DOLORES: This isn't an examination, Joe.

JOE: Really?

DOLORES: Really.

JOE: Maybe it would help if I knew what you were looking for.

DOLORES: Honestly?
    I can't tell you. Mostly it's 'not fitting'.
    Some wrong detail.

     Pause.

DOLORES: So you wake up, you feel cold in your toes,
     everywhere is covered in glass. What do you think? Mrs
     Tremarco catches the full force of whatever it was, what did
     you think, your first thought.

JOE: Honestly?
     I thought it was the sea, gushing in.
     I'd lost my shoes, you see;
     paddling.
     Skegness on holiday or something.

DOLORES: Skegness, the beach resort.

          Beat.

JOE: Are you sure you're the right person for this, because…

DOLORES: I belong to this city Joe, if that's your concern.
     I'm raising my kids in this town.

          Beat.

     You lost your shoes. Not unusual,
     that happens with a blast like this.
     Often.

JOE: I was face down, over by the
     Reading Room in this, as I said, ocean of glass.
     Shards of glass
     one of our more feeble poets would have it.

          Pause.

DOLORES: Can you show me on the plan here?
     L12. Photocopying and Resources – right?

JOE: Actually it was a Reading Room.
     A few shelves, chairs.
     It was close, I realised I could –
     I thought swim but I must have meant crawl – over to it.

DOLORES: To the Reading Room.

JOE: Across the glass. I could
     pick my way. If I was careful.
     I could find shelter there

hopefully
I could find my way out.
before…

DOLORES: Before?

JOE: The ceiling was almost down, all angles
The floor…
Whatever was happening, hadn't finished happening.
I remember thinking that.

>   *Pause.*

DOLORES: Why was that?

JOE: Why hadn't it stopped?

DOLORES: Why did you think that it hadn't?

>   *Pause.*

JOE: Things were moving, still, maybe.
Falling.

DOLORES: Or you heard other explosions.

>   *Pause.*

Odd, don't you think?
A reading room.
out of context somehow.

JOE: It's a room full of books.

DOLORES: That's what I mean.

JOE: There's nothing odd about books.

DOLORES: It's unusual to have a room full of books
a Reading Room
in a busy office, in a company, in a city like this
Don't you think?
Nowadays.

JOE: You mean because Google has sushi bars and ping-pong
tables?

DOLORES: Maybe.

JOE: We were old-fashioned innovators:
    a different kind of firm, a new way of working
    Freeing up the creative mind
    Life and work, the spirit, a nurturing environment
    We had family days in the beginning
    Hot air balloon rides
    All kinds of stuff

DOLORES: Balloon rides?

JOE: Parties.
    Steven and Ahmed wanted it that way
    imagine, discovering life could be different.
    A different way of doing things.

DOLORES: Steven and Ahmed are the founders of the company.

JOE: Yes, Along with Michael.

DOLORES: Michael who was forced out early on.

      Pause.

DOLORES: Go on.

JOE: I went to one party at a huge house in the country and the
    pond,
    the lake, was entirely covered in balloons, small ones
    tethered I suppose…

DOLORES: I meant what happened next.

JOE: Next we got the new building.
    Along with the restaurant,
    there was the Reading Room.

      Beat.

DOLORES: You mean the canteen. L29.

JOE: No, a restaurant, with a two-star chef. Flat whites, light
    lunches. Avocado.
    Very good lunches, actually.

      Pause.

DOLORES: So you headed for the Reading Room.

JOE: I slid over to it.
  A lot of books were destroyed,
  Modern languages was gone, fiction in tatters,
  The poetry section was untouched, obviously
  If you'd met some of our interns…(that's obvious)
  Reference was solid, oddly.

DOLORES: And you noticed all this.

JOE: I did.

DOLORES: And then?

JOE: Then I thought – sellotape. No use on books that size
  even if I had more than one roll, but my
  shirt was shredded so I pulled strips of cloth from my shirt
  Tied them together and
  I strapped a book to each
  foot.

> *Beat.*

  I don't remember which books
  is that a problem?

DOLORES: Not important, probably.

JOE: Thick ones, anyway.
  The Complete Works and Johnson's Dictionary I should think.
  I remember being lop-sided when I walked so
  it may have been the King James Bible and Parker's guide.
  Funny.
  Most people would remember a thing like that.

DOLORES: Most people.

JOE: I don't remember anything.

DOLORES: But that's how you got out of the building.

JOE: It's how I crossed the floor
  then I banged my head
  I was unconscious again.

DOLORES: For how long this time?

JOE: No idea.
>Once you're at work, times not your own.
>It's not as if I'm tall, especially.
>Some of the joists from the floor above had…
>And I was now…
>I was a giant
>Striding over a sea of glass like a colossus,
>aided only by the jewels of British culture.

DOLORES: Until you hit your head.

JOE: Yes.

DOLORES:

JOE:

DOLORES: Literature can be elevating, they say.

JOE: They do say that.

>*Pause.*

DOLORES: Okay.
>Well thankyou Joe
>it must be painful trawling through all this stuff

JOE: It is.

DOLORES: I get that.

JOE: You've drawn all the conclusions you need, have you?

DOLORES: I think so.

>*Beat.*

>You're lucky to be alive, Joe, I know that much.
>Lucky to live in a place where alarms go off, fire trucks come.
>Breathing equipment when it arrives, works, usually.

JOE: Lucky to live in a western city, you mean. Where we're protected.

>*Beat.*

DOLORES: We're just trying to work out what went on here exactly.

Do better.

> *Beat.*

DOLORES: God knows what we'll do if they target this place.
No one's getting far on
the Police Gazette and a copy of Reader's Wives, right Joe?

JOE:

JOE: Not if.

DOLORES: Pardon me?

JOE: Not if
you are targeted.

DOLORES: Honestly?
I try not to think about that.

JOE: You should. We should be alert. All of us.
What is it?
Put the kid's breakfast bowls out
Packet of cereal, no sharp corners
Hope for the best?

DOLORES: Something like that.

> *Beat.*

DOLORES: I turn each bowl half a turn anti-clockwise
if you want to know.
Kind of a rewind the clock thing
Maybe my children will get a few more seconds if
they do get caught up.
But then I come to work and I apply reason.
Like I said this is my city too.

> *Pause.*

JOE: I thought I spoke to the bomber
before the blast

DOLORES: Oh?

JOE: He explained some things, tried.
Wanted me to know…

DOLORES: Woah woah.
　　When was this exactly?

　　　　Beat.

JOE: He was downstairs. In the atrium.

DOLORES: And you were what – down there too?

JOE: No, I was in the office.

　　　　Beat.

JOE: He wanted to tell me why he hated us
　　How it felt to be doing what he was
　　doing
　　Had done by then. He was local
　　Loved the building
　　Something about his brother.

DOLORES: Right.

JOE: I told him to fuck off

　　Obviously.

DOLORES: Obviously.

JOE:

DOLORES: The bomber was several floors down Joe – eighteen
　　in fact.

JOE: You're saying I imagined he had things to say to me?

DOLORES: I'm saying it's hard to see how the conversation could
　　happen in the real
　　world.

JOE: Is that a good thing?

　　　　Pause. She glances at her watch

DOLORES: We're conducting a very thorough review, Joe. I
　　should call you again about
　　this, when you're feeling more collected.

JOE: I'm very collected. Thankyou.

DOLORES: Can I get you a taxi now?

> *Beat.*

JOE: Yes. Thankyou.

> *He pads his pockets for a plastic carrier bag, and finds one.*

I get car sick if you can believe that
Balance is…
Still,
better than the alternative.

DOLORES: Tube will be back soon, one hundred percent.

JOE: Sitting at home
Not imagining.
They're arresting dog-walkers now
Did you hear?
for not clearing up the crap.
People are terrified to be on the street
Heads down, scoot by, scurry home
No time for poop patrol.
Arresting people for being scared shitless
Fucking brilliant.
That's what the city needs, right?
A stronger hand.
that's what the analysts all say
is it?
at the top level.

DOLORES: Like I said Joe, we'll be in touch.

> *Pause.*

Want me to go first?

> *Lights.*

FIGHTING BACK

The sound of ripping paper leads us into the scene.

JOE is surrounded by torn up books. He is tearing them apart.

RUSHA: *(Off, calling.)* It's me.

JOE: If that's who I think it is – come in.
    Anyone else
    fuck off.

RUSHA: *(off)* Hell- o-o

JOE: In here.

        RUSHA enters.

RUSHA: Wow.
    Busy.

JOE: Miss Murthy. Mind the gaff.
    I'm learning to agree with the rest of the world,
    A little poetry goes a long way.

RUSHA: Wow.

JOE: Did you bring me ammunition?

        She is carrying a box of books, which she puts down.

RUSHA: Having a clear out anyway, so…

        He pulls out a copy.

JOE: Ah. The Star Wars Annual.
    Interesting vintage…
    With free Princess Leia poster -
    Perfect.

        He rips it up.

RUSHA: Impressive.

JOE: A new meaning for the phrase ripping yarns

RUSHA:

JOE: Anyway. How's it going, for you. Rusha.

RUSHA: Fine. You, Joe?

JOE: Good. Excellent.
   Well, you know.

RUSHA:

JOE: I watched your clips, by the way, finally. On the…thing.

RUSHA: Ah.

JOE: Impressive. Locking yobby teenagers in a storecupboard

RUSHA: I am such an idiot.

JOE: It was a close call.

RUSHA: The road menders outside – they kept going that noise, I
   thought there was shooting … (we were being attacked).

JOE: You said.

   Pause.

JOE: You okay?

RUSHA: Fine.

   Beat.

JOE: They can sound like machine guns.
   (The drills.)

RUSHA: Right.
   They call me the Take Cover Teacher.

   Beat.

RUSHA: So
   time I made some trouble in the real world.
   I thought you'd be interested.
   There's a whole crowd going down.

JOE: Good. Excellent.
   Just my thing.
   To the library.

RUSHA: It's not far, we can walk or…

JOE: Good, local library. Clue's in the name.

>   *Beat.*

RUSHA: I never knew you were actually in there,
>   in the Beer Glass.

JOE: The biggest commercial building in the city.
>   Advice to my countrymen.
>   My troubles are your troubles, very soon.
>   Unless…
>   Bloody road repairs, eh?
>   Meanwhile the good guys want to close the library.

RUSHA: It's a bit of a passion of mine, protest.

JOE: SO, this is the prototype. I call it
>   the Dust Jacket.

>   *He has made a jacket with pages or clumps of pages taped*
>   *together. He slips it on.*

JOE: How do I look?
>   Hesitation.

RUSHA: Honestly?
>   No, I can't say.

JOE:

RUSHA: It looks a bit bomb-vesty

JOE: Bombvesty.
>   that's a word is it?

RUSHA: Sorry

JOE: Rapey, bombvesty…

RUSHA: I said, I'm sorry.

>   *Beat.*

JOE: No – honesty's essential
>   where fashion's concerned.

>   *Beat.*

JOE: Bombvesty.
> That may be taken as provocative.
> What about epaulettes?

> *He places a book in position on his shoulder.*

JOE: Too military?

RUSHA: Better.

JOE: I was thinking Tin Man, you see, only books.

RUSHA: And a heart

JOE: Ah. Might be the missing link.

> *Beat.*

RUSHA: You're still up for doing a speech for us
> are you?

JOE: Sure.
> I made you one, by the way.

> *He produces a jacket for her, she puts it on.*

JOE: Sometimes I imagine the smallest space I could fit in and
want to be there
> completely apart so I never have to see another living soul
again.
> I swing from that to feeling I should be out there peeling off
my skin
> showing my insides to anyone and everyone and saying this is
me do your
> worst if you really think I'm so different from you
> Go ahead, take a shot, press the button, there's nothing to stop
you.

> *Pause.*

RUSHA: I was thinking a speech about libraries.

JOE: I'll save it for the stand up.
> 'Taking Terrorism Personally'
> I might call it.
> This is ideal preparation.

'Books Saved My Life But Also Gave Me Amnesia.'

RUSHA: How's that going?

JOE: How's what going?

RUSHA: You're good.
　　That really happened, did it?
　　The books on the feet thing? You said at the meeting...

JOE: It came back to me.
　　It may have come back.
　　Hard to tell.
　　We all need some kind of story,
　　To explain things.

RUSHA: We do.

　　We should go.

JOE: Wait
　　so let me try this alright.

> *He tears a page from one of the clumps of pages fastened to his chest. He prepares himself to read, and lets James' words cast their spell.*

...the room looked empty as only a room can look in Paris, of a fine afternoon, when the faint murmer of the huge collective life, carried on out of doors, strays among scattered objects even as a summer air idles in a lonely garden.

Do you know who that's from,
madam?

RUSHA: I...
　　I don't really read much.

JOE: Henry James – the greatest writer ever.
　　Failed playwright.
　　You should ask, What's that got to do with me?

RUSHA: Sorry:
　　What's that got to do with me?

JOE: Nothing – maybe.

But you can find out because his books are right here (in your
library).
Imagine
discovering, as a modern woman, you have anything in
common
anything at all
with an elderly, white, long dead, American man of letters.
How is that
possible? Because
the genius of Henry James is to bottle the essence of life
The genius of the library is to stock him.
Joni Mitchell had it wrong, you see
It's not sex that's touching souls it's books
Once this library's gone
do you have money madam?

RUSHA: Some

JOE: If you don't have money
    and sex with strangers is not…available
    or appropriate, go to the library.
    They're run by volunteers these days
    Why is that?
    A library is a battery charged with kindness and trust.
    You don't borrow a book because you paid for it
    there's no exchange. Ask, here,
    and you receive.
    If you have no money,
    No idea how learning works
    Let the bookshelf lead you. Go ahead.
    Make whatever connections you want –
    Local history and the thoughts of Chairman Mao
    Female genital mutilation and landscape gardening
    You don't have to justify what you read,
    What you think about it – to anyone!
    Freedom!
    Read the paper, read nothing
    Stay all day if you want, stay warm
    Stay till your mum finishes her shift somewhere.
    In Denmark they tried a human library

You could borrow a goth for twenty minutes
See the world through panda eyes!
In Hong Kong they have Thought Debates
In Chicago they just opened sixteen new libraries
      Where?
At the edges, between silos of black and white
Why?

RUSHA: Work it out.
    In the library.

JOE: We should open more libraries.
    Every high street should have a portal
    The mass of human experience is everyone's birthright
    How can we learn if we can't get at it?
    If we are going to survive
    It's our duty and our privilege to help each other
    Touch souls
    And we should do that, all of us, every day, for more than
    one hundred and forty characters at a fucking time.
    That's why you must help save *your* library.

        Pause.

RUSHA: Honestly?
    That's brilliant.

        Beat.

JOE: Maybe just ask them to sign the petition.

RUSHA: Maybe.
    Good.

JOE: Excellent.

JOE: Now I think about it
    it was love, anyway, the touching souls thing
    not sex. Some old lover had surely touched hers.

RUSHA: Right.

        Beat.

RUSHA: You still want to do this do you?

If it gets too much
If we get too much attention
I'll get you away.

JOE: Thankyou.
I'll be fine.
And if not
Let's share a flashback and murder everyone
Sorry.
Losing a reading room and a perfectly decent library in one
lifetime
Not on my watch.

RUSHA: we can get the 32 if you like
Or we can walk…?

JOE: Bus. Right at the lights,
Four stops down

JOE breathes deeply. He takes out his plastic bag.

JOE: I once knew a man who thought he could fly.
Did I tell you?

RUSHA: This is another one.

JOE: Genuinely. He was a banker.
Gareth.
We used to play squash together
when I played squash.
One afternoon he walked straight through the window
floor above mine
nineteen floors

RUSHA: That's awful.

JOE: I was in the Reading Room.
I could see he was right, briefly.

RUSHA: I'll see you downstairs.

RUSHA exits.

JOE: That's what…(he said)

JOE smooths out his sick bag, takes a deep breath,

JOE: Attack attack attack

> *He follows.*

> *Lights.*

PREPARING THE STUDENT

Soundtrack from a cartoon movie brings us into the scene.

A room on a university campus in North Africa. FAROUK is standing, watching a television, surrounded by books, scattered on the floor. AMNA waits to enter.

AMNA: Sir?

FAROUK: Yes?

AMNA: I am Amna.

FAROUK: Please.
  Are you familiar with this film, Amna?

AMNA: No, sir. I do not believe such films are halal.

> *Beat.*

FAROUK: My daughter says it helps my grandson to learn to
  speak English. American.
  Believers can learn from the morality of the story. All the
  toys working together. And the second iteration is better
  than the first. Did you see the first in this sequence?

AMNA: No sir.

FAROUK: Nor me. But I heard that.

> *Beat.*

AMNA: You must pardon the devastation. Collateral damage
  from our friends the builders; a bookshelf falls from the
  wall – unimaginable confusion results.

> *Through the rest of the scene he clears the books into a
> cardboard box(es).*

FAROUK: Is the work at the hostel completed now?

AMNA: Yes sir, the refurbishments are all complete.

> *Beat.*

Sir, my friend has died. Your student Houida has been
murdered.

Beat.

FAROUK: Oh?

AMNA: A drone swooped from the sky. No one was murdered but Houida – she was just helping with children at a wedding.

FAROUK: I am sorry.
These are terrible times for the pure of heart.

AMNA: Houida had the purest heart of any person I knew.

Beat.

None of us can count the days we have been given.

Beat.

FAROUK: Houida – the athlete. She was a big-hearted girl, certainly.

AMNA: Yessir, she was.

FAROUK: She made friends with a student from the south.
You are from the South of course.
The height, the accent. Also, something refined in the articulation of your ideas.

AMNA: My father originated from the south, sir.

FAROUK: So you are Christian.

Beat.

AMNA: I have chosen a different path for myself. Since I came to the college…
Houida showed me it is vital to live a full and useful life.
I have been Moslem for more than two months now.

FAROUK: That is a considerable choice you have made.

AMNA: I am in dialogue with the imam, sir. He has helped my understanding. Until now, the hardest steps were behind me.

FAROUK: I'm sure the imam will help further in this time of mourning.

Pause.

FAROUK: Your work at the college is good. Actually excellent.

AMNA: I work hard, sir. I wish to honour the Prophet, peace be upon him.

FAROUK: Or perhaps the work is easy for you.

>   *Beat.*

Enlighten me about your situation; is there a television you can watch? In the common room, at the hostel where you live.

AMNA: No sir. We are allowed to listen to the radio.

FAROUK: Do you listen to the news on the radio?

AMNA: Yessir. That is how I first heard about the attack. Houida always preferred the programme from the mosque.

FAROUK: Then you have witnessed this latest phase of history. Europe draining Africa of its people. You are aware of this phenomena?

AMNA: I am sir.

FAROUK: What is your opinion of the phenomena, from the theological and historical perspective?

AMNA: I am not a student of history, sir.

>   *Beat.*

It is regrettable; there is a general lack of faith, the loss of men and women who might otherwise build the future. The word 'draining' is well chosen. I wish more people would stay. I wish more people would serve the caliphate.

>   *Beat.*

FAROUK: Surely, it is a believer's duty to serve the Prophet, peace be upon him.

AMNA: Our faith should be manifest on earth, sir. To be a true and happy home for the people – this is the meaning of the caliphate; soon, as in the former times, the whole world will live happily under *sharia*.

119

Beat.

FAROUK: From the greatest trial comes great reward.
Permit me to tell you something from the hadiths, and also
my own experience. Sadness should not be entertained for
more than a season.
I don't say this to be unkind.
Always, good can come from bad *inshallah.*

He removes the DVD from the machine.

I am like you, Amna, a believer. I have wished happiness
for our world, since I was the smallest child. Later I
realised that cannot be. Never, until the world of lies,
deception and murder that we hear about on the radio, the
television, is gone, a world that enslaves foolish people.
Europe, America, these powers know nothing of peace.
In Paris, London…even in Berlin, I myself have seen
believers snared in a trap of the west's making – happiness
sought in things, in material possessions – some are rich,
true, but so many have nothing, not even the comfort
of real faith. In Europe today, it is the believer who is
despised and rejected.
This is the change the caliphate must bring. Happiness for
all people. But perhaps to pursue such a future does not
interest you. You want a husband, children, this is normal
… (for a girl of your age)

AMNA: No, sir, I have brains. To be a wife, to be a mother is a
faithful life, but … (not something I want for myself).
I have chosen to serve the future with all of my strength.

Beat.

FAROUK: Did you ever travel to Europe, yourself Amna?

AMNA: No sir. I don't desire to live such a life.

FAROUK: Of course. You are living faithfully …

AMNA: Please. I am a person with a zealous heart.

Pause.

FAROUK: We should talk again, Amna. There are people I have contact with – computers are not in themselves haraam any more than a television, or a radio – perhaps these brothers might offer their advice.

AMNA: I would be pleased to receive it sir.

FAROUK: Consider the direction of your life, Amna. To have a friend is a blessing, but before Allah we must all give account. Consider what you will do for the zealous faith you have been given.
Keep this. A gift.

He gives her the DVD.

AMNA: I don't have a player sir.

FAROUK: If we serve history, Amna, we become the players.

AMNA: Is that from another film sir?

Beat.

Thank you.

Lights.

PARKLIFE.

A bench, in a city park. An ice cream van's mad music heard off – 'O, O Antonio', or 'Greensleeves'. NO NAME II, head-scarved, pushing a pram. She sits. There is no one about. She stands up takes a few steps forward.

NO NAME II: Raise the flag.

>*A moment. Louder.*

RAISE THE FLAG.

>*Bang.*

>*A bomb explodes. Silence.*

ALMOST A MODEST PROPOSAL NEAR THE LIBRARY

Traffic noise. Outside, on the street, not far from the park.

RUSHA stands waiting, still wearing her dust jacket, smoking.

JOE enters in high spirits, and with cups of coffee.

JOE: A good afternoon's protest – and a just reward.
Thank god for Bean Hunter.

RUSHA: Okay over here?

JOE: Fine – no seats left anyway.

They sip their coffee.

JOE: It comes down to snobbery
Probably.
If I'd chosen thin books
Mills and Boon, Star Wars
I'd never have been such a colossus
wouldn't have banged my head

RUSHA: That's why they call it low brow.

JOE: Good. Or Haynes manuals –
Do they still do Haynes manuals?
Ford Cortinas, Hillman Imps?

RUSHA: Don't think so
My dad says that's what's
wrong with the world;
Nobody fixes things.

JOE: This is the dad with cancer?

RUSHA: Step dad

JOE: He'd know I suppose.

RUSHA: He's thin now
'a prune where a plum once grew'

JOE: You can download a manual for anything now
Washer. Pacemaker.

who bothers,
Be like that with bodies soon.
Throw one away, get another.
That why you're smoking?

RUSHA: Probably won't stick with it
Another of my passing fancies.
I'm not really given to passing fancies, I just…

Pause.

RUSHA: Can I ask you something?

JOE: Sure.

RUSHA: You and Jackie
The lady who died in the
Beer Glass…

JOE: No. No definite article.
Something else I have to learn.
There were thirty-six ladies.
Ten from our floor, two passing by on the pavement, lots
from accounts
Eighty-seven people in all.

RUSHA: It's only her you talk about.

Beat.

JOE: Honestly? She mothered me.
When I started.
I liked it.
Someone to have a glass of white wine with
when the world was shit.
I was a bit of an island for her too I think
a holiday at home a
what do they call it?
A staycation
Jackie said I was an island, as a person, but that an island
can mean isolation or it can be a safe place in the middle
of traffic
That was Britain too, she said – and I was its perfect citizen.

Pause.

Jackie was the last really good person on earth.
No offence.

RUSHA: I was married for a while. Can't really believe it.

JOE: I'm a glacial person now.
Like glass
That's what happens to the stuff islands are made of
Heat sand up, out pops glass.
Frosted, in my case, obviously.

RUSHA: I miss it. Being close to someone.

JOE: Did you hear something? A shout.

> *They listen. The mad ice-cream van music, distant.*

RUSHA: It's an ice-cream…(van)

JOE: There!

> *A bomb explodes in the park.*

Jesus.

RUSHA: Stay still Joe. Stay calm.

JOE: Shit. SHIT!!

> *He tears at his jacket, beats his head, crumples, she comforts him.*

RUSHA: Sssshhhhhh.

> *Lights down.*

SUNDAY IN THE PARK WITH JOE

A park. A mangled park bench – just about usable. Police incident tape is being rolled up.

DOLORES.

DOLORES: Schools make sense.
  I get that.
  Boys and girls, in and out of each others' pants.
  Just learning together, that's provocation.
  Subway? Footfall. Also the map, the goddam tube map,
  like they've gotta
  join the dots or something.
  The Beer Glass? Temple to the barbarian west.
  This?
  Ducks.
  When did ducks become the enemy?
  That's why we're meeting here, right? Showing me how far
  behind the curve we are?

> *JOE has entered.*

JOE: Here?

DOLORES: Right here
  Bench survived – just about. Didn't even take the fun-
  runners out. Seriously, this is a big no-fit.
  A woman – a girl – walks into a park, headscarf naturally,
  pram for cover.
  First time, we figure, okay, someone is fearful. They bale
  out, it's
  an unstable property – kaboom.
  This one is the fifth, parkwise.
  Only she is destroyed.
  What is that? Do they hate their women so damn much?
  Do they have so
  many followers they can toss them away like this?

JOE:

> *Beat.*

DOLORES: Listen, I heard about your group, Joe. I just want to say I think it's great.

> *Beat.*

Great name you all came up with: B.B.A.; Bomb Bait Anonymous. The famous gallows humour, right?

JOE:

DOLORES: Where I come from therapy's no disgrace. Actually we boast about it.

JOE: We're survivors. A few… over-reactors, getting ourselves together. So our voices can be heard.

DOLORES: Good. That's positive.

> *Beat.*

DOLORES: Joe, we didn't get on so well before.

JOE:

DOLORES: You thought you had some kind of communication with the bomber. At the Beer Glass.

JOE: He was nineteen floors away. It didn't happen.

DOLORES:

JOE:

DOLORES: Okay – Honestly? That was then this is now.

JOE:

DOLORES: I would value your input.
Tell me. First thoughts. This whole park thing.

JOE: I remembered something, from before. It *was* the King James Bible. Not
Parker's guide, birds probably, on the left foot. 'We wrestle not against
flesh and blood but against wickedness in high places.' For them, I mean.
That's how it is.

DOLORES: Well they are taking plenty of flesh and blood with them.

Take days to get this poor girl down from the trees.

JOE: This is the English bloody Channel. The Breton Sea. Your war on hate is The

Flag's war on Peace. War on the mash up –

cosmopolitanism, actually. There's

plenty here who don't like that. War on the city, being who we are, living how we do. Parks?

Where does anyone go to calm themselves – even when we're old and can't get out?

DOLORES: I dunno. The pub?

JOE: Farming programmes. Since they've been ill, for my parents? Sheep, morning till night. Walks in the lakes with Bobby and Charlie.

If you *can* get out, but live in a city – this is it. Room for everyone, safe for children, free – you should bring yours down.

Free to not always be alert. That's Britain: a safe place in the middle of traffic.

How can we function without this?

But that's not where resources will go now, is it; parks, duckponds.

Fences, walls, submarines

we invest in all the wrong weapons.

> *Pause.*

Your turn. What's the plan, Dolores?

DOLORES: It's not clear yet. Internment I guess.

JOE: Internment!?

DOLORES: Not an easy job, we're not talking about a handful of people here.

JOE: For who? Where?

DOLORES: Don't react Joe, nothing's been confirmed. There'll be a point system.

Croyden's being considered.
Croyden's being considered.

JOE: This is a joke.

DOLORES: Should be Mayfair. No one wants to be punitive,
right?
At first anyway.

JOE: Oh for god'sake.

He makes to exit.

DOLORES: Regimes are falling all round the globe.
The Flag gets control of real toys? Peace, Hate, call it what
you like, it's a war. We have to think vertically now.

JOE: ?

DOLORES: It won't be bird-spotting my kids get into. Will it.

JOE: So do something, before they fall. Make spaces where
people can be, to mix and think and waste time and play,
have a barbeque – bring back stories, help us be free in the
head, for a while. People don't need libraries? – okay, fine
– *if* they already know their way round the world, *if* they
know how the system works, maybe you're right. Can they
imagine new things?
Can they see how things can be changed?

DOLORES: You think we have time to worry about books
now?
Everyone says libraries are Kindergartens these days
anyhow.

JOE: I'M NOT JUST TALKING ABOUT BOOKS.

Beat.

DOLORES: Christ.

JOE: What are you doing?

*DOLORES punches her phone. Only her side of the conversation
is heard.*

DOLORES: *(Phone)* It's me. Go down the list; libraries and museums…
…Well they're public spaces and there's kids there. Code 5, close them down…
…Fuck the local authority…

> *Pause.*

Right, okay…
No…no I get that. I'll come in.
Look. Find me a politician, would you?

> *She shuts off the phone.*

Fire meets fire – that in the scriptures too?

JOE:

DOLORES: Someone doused an imam with something. We think chip oil. Went up like a torch.
We're fighting for his life now.
It's a beginning.

> *DOLORES exits. JOE, alone, looks about, then sits on what is left of the park bench, sitting where we saw the bomber sat.*
>
> *A group of school kids approach, singing a football chant – we hear them before we see them. NIALL, PARVENDRA and LORNA – are larking about, and drinking. PARVENDRA is pushing or riding a bike, LORNA drinking from a can. They are boisterous, dominating the whole space, arms aloft, singing as loud as they can, oblivious to JOE. NIALL might even stand on the end of the bench JOE is sitting on.*

LORNA: You're such a dick.

PARVENDRA: Wanker.

> *Etc. – They drift away happily, still singing, laughing, just larking about.*
>
> *JOE is left alone, his smile draining.*
>
> *Lights.*

TO INFINITY…

A low level hum brings us into the scene. AMNA on a chair, wearing a flying suit, and a headscarf. She is reading a book. Enter FAROUK.

FAROUK: Good evening Amna – Day of days.

AMNA: Sir – They allowed you to come here.

FAROUK: I was granted special dispensation.

> *Beat.*

It's good to see you are still studying. The Quran always brings a light to the eyes.

> *She tosses the book onto the floor.*

AMNA: Not the Holy Quran, sir. We just have training manuals. A good navigation officer has so much lodged inside her head.

FAROUK: God forgive me, I am so very proud of your achievements.

> *AMNA zips up her flying suit, extracts her flying helmet from under the chair.*

AMNA: I never dreamed I could do this, even to be considered for instruction.

FAROUK: The Commander agrees with me – those brains are so agile.
You discovered your purpose, Amna: To infinity and beyond!

> *Their smiles are interrupted. Tannoy, very clipped.*

TANNOY: Three minutes.

> *Noise of jet engines massively increases. AMNA makes to exit, FAROUK dons his ear defenders, the noise is really overpowering. AMNA checks her exit.*

AMNA: WE MAY NOT RETURN.

> *She knows she is not communicating. She tries again.*

THE WEST HAS STRONG DEFENCES.

He can't hear a thing – shakes his head.

FAROUK: NOTHING.

She gives up, salutes him with the slogan:

AMNA: RAISE THE FLAG.

FAROUK: RAISE THE FLAG. RAZE THE CITY.

AMNA: Raze the city.

AMNA exits.

Alone, FAROUK turns to see the book on the floor. He picks it up, places it respectfully on the chair, and exits.

Bare stage, just the chair, and the noise.

TANNOY: Two minutes.

The roar increases.

Silence.

THE END

On being open.

Give or take the *Prologue* and the scene called *To Infinity...,* the scenes in *Always Orange* can be presented in any order; in theatre parlance, the order is 'open'.

If the playwright is alive, a company usually has little choice over the ordering of events in a play; except in very experimental or immersive shows, what the playwright puts at the front, stays there; what is revealed last, will be the final thing that is presented. For the audience, this is the cause of much suffering. Unlike the books they were reading on the train to the theatre, an audience cannot flick over the boring bits to get to the meat of the play. If they could, most plays would be shorter.

For this reason, deciding the order in which the action is presented has always seemed to me to be one of the key tools in a playwright's artfully casual-looking shoulder-bag – one of the main means of story-telling. What we see first often conditions how we interpret what follows; what comes last, may cause us to re-evaluate everything that went before. Mess with that order, and you may seriously weaken the analysis being offered, as well as confuse the story in a distracting way.

So why risk the wisdom of the playwright, and the power of the play, by declaring the scene order open?

For myself, the answer is simple: it feels interesting, and creative, and allows any subsequent artistic team to wrestle with some of the issues we wrestled with at The Other Place in the summer of 2016. The decision to declare the play open – albeit in our qualified sense – arose from the observation in rehearsal that the scenes in this play don't tumble one into the other, or cause each other to be, in any simple or consistent way. We could shuffle the order, and still tell essentially the same fractured story in a comprehensible way, though with slightly different effects.

We chose to go with the order in which the scenes are presented here partly out of principle. Following *Prologue* with the scene called *Jackie's Last Day* means that the play begins with a real-world situation – a workplace 'leaving do' – followed very shortly by a second real-world event which throws that 'norm' into confusion. Joe's head and confidence is scrambled not because he is by nature a confused person, but because of an immensely traumatic event that happens in the physical world. When we put *Jackie's Last Day* towards the end of the play the story still works perfectly, but causes us – perhaps – to read Joe's confusion as a trick of memory – a product purely of his psychological state.

The choice of order is also though, about context – the state the world is in when the play is produced. The order in which the scenes are given here is the order that I as playwright, in conversation with director, AD and dramaturg, decided made most sense in July 2016, in Stratford-upon-Avon in the UK, in a production marking the very exciting re-opening of The Other Place. Your context is different, and maybe a different order will make more sense to your creative team. Knock yourself out. *Prologue* is the prologue, and *To Infinity…* is a kind of coda. Apart from that, over to you.

FG